*Five Women
Who Loved
Love*

The title and author's name are presented
on the cover in Japanese characters.

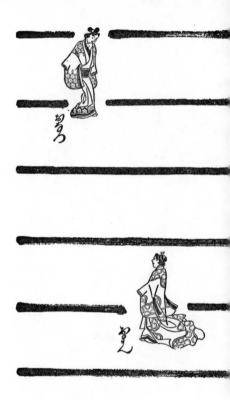

with a background essay by
RICHARD LANE

and the 17th-century illustrations by
YOSHIDA HAMBEI

CHARLES E. TUTTLE COMPANY : PUB-

Five Women Who Loved Love

by *IHARA SAIKAKU*

translated by WM. THEODORE DE BARY

LISHERS : RUTLAND VERMONT : TOKYO JAPAN

Representatives
British Isles & Continental Europe:
SIMON & SCHUSTER INTERNATIONAL GROUP, *London*
Australasia: BOOKWISE INTERNATIONAL
1 Jeanes Street, Beverley, 5009, South Australia

Published by the Charles E. Tuttle Company, Inc.
of Rutland, Vermont & Tokyo, Japan
with editorial offices at
Suido 1-chome, 2-6, Bunkyo-ku, Tokyo

Copyright in Japan, 1956
by Charles E. Tuttle Co., Inc.

Library of Congress Catalog
Card No. 55-10619

International Standard Book No. 0-8048-0184-3

First edition, 1956
Twenty-fifth printing, 1988

Printed in Japan

TO

FANNY

Contents

Illustrations

*The illustrations throughout the book are facsimile repro-
ductions, reduced to about sixty percent of the original
size, of the woodblock prints appearing in the original
Japanese edition of* Five Women Who Loved Love, *dated
1686. The artist was Yoshida Hambei, the leading illustrator of the Kyóto-Osaka region in Saikaku's day. Illustrations for the five stories will be found on the following
pages*

Foreword

In translating *Five Women Who Loved Love* I have tried to preserve as much as possible of Saikaku's rich poetry, exuberant wit, and economy of language. To do this is difficult in any case, difficult in much the same way as it would be to translate James Joyce's *Finnegans Wake* into everyday English. Having bound Saikaku's feet with such prose, I thought it a poor idea to encumber him further with extensive annotation. Brief notes are given where necessary to help the reader keep up with Saikaku, but not to sidetrack him on points of literary or historical interest, which are indeed plentiful.

Since I first performed this pleasant experiment in translation in 1946, there has been a great revival of interest in Saikaku's works among the Japanese. Compared with what went before, a vast amount of critical scholarship on Saikaku has been produced in the last several years. There is even a special periodical entitled *Saikaku Studies* being published in Tokyo, of which eight volumes have already appeared. Fortunately, this research is being supplemented by the efforts of Western students to make Saikaku better known outside his homeland. In particular I should like to mention the work of Mr. Richard Lane, who has kindly provided an essay on the background and historical sources of Saikaku's *Five Women* for this edition; and also of Professor Howard Hibbett, of the University of California at Los Angeles. My own translation has not enjoyed the full fruits of this late harvest of scholarship, but several friends whose judgment in these matters counts for more than my own have persuaded me that its publication may still fill a need among the growing number of readers seeking a first acquaintance with Saikaku—a need heightened by recent scholarly interest, which confirms rather than abrogates the central position in Japanese literature of his greatest works.

The text for this translation of *Koshoku gonin onna* has come from the series *Nihon bungaku taikei,* Vol. IV, *Ihara Saikaku shu* (Works of Ihara Saikaku), edited by Sasakawa Shuro and published in Tokyo in 1925. Although originally printed with numerous expurgations, the copy used here had been rendered complete through reference to an unexpurgated text by the Kokusai Bunka Shinkokai, which forwarded it to the Japan Institute in New York before World

War II. Doubtful points have been checked against a more recent version edited by Professor Teruoka Yasutaka (*Koshoku gonin onna hyoshaku,* Tokyo, 1953).

The writing of this translation was suggested to me by Mr. Ryusaku Tsunoda, long a student of Saikaku, who has recently retired after many years of distinguished service as Curator of the Japanese Collection at Columbia University. Throughout my work Mr. Tsunoda was constantly helpful and encouraging. Mr. Lane has also put me heavily in his debt by reading the manuscript and making many helpful suggestions and corrections, particularly in regard to the first of these stories. I am grateful as well to Professors Donald L. Keene and Harold G. Henderson, Sir George Sansom, Mr. Robert S. Gerdy, Miss Anna Horton, and my wife, Fanny Brett de Bary, for the assistance each of them gave me in the project.

W. T. DE B.

Introduction

Five Women Who Loved Love was written by a citizen of Osaka for the amusement of the townspeople in the new commercial centers of seventeenth-century Japan. From the few surviving records of Ihara Saikaku we know that he was not only a popular novelist but also a poet of wide reputation in his own day, a playwright and commentator on theatre life, and also something of a vagabond who had closely observed life as it was lived in parts of the country other than his own. Being so cosmopolitan, he was all the more truly a citizen of Osaka. The things that fascinated him in his native city he also found in others—back alleys and slums as well as gay theatres and teahouses; beggars, peddlers, and the lowliest prostitutes, along with merchant princes and famous courtesans. But in writing about them as he did, with such a rare combination of sympathy and detachment, Saikaku gave expression to a feeling of which the inhabitants of Osaka were probably more conscious than other townspeople: that they were citizens with a new importance to society and a new outlook on the world, one which showed the way to a richer and happier life than medieval Japan had known. This came to be known as the *chonin-do*, "the way of the townspeople," in contrast to *bushido*, "'the way of the warrior," which has been so widely publicized in recent years that it has come to appear to many as the sole embodiment of Japanese tradition.

If Saikaku, as spokesman for the new citizenry, did not compose a "Marseillaise" to inspire his fellow townsmen in a struggle against the old order, it is partly because fighting was one of the things they wished to free themselves from. They were engaged together, not in a class struggle, but in pursuit of individual happiness—something for which little allowance had been made in the stern and unsparing life of medieval fighting men. Indeed, this pursuit, so taken for granted in our part of the world today, was almost revolutionary in its implications for a society which had long lived as though in a graveyard, overcast by the seemingly endless tragedy of war, haunted in its literature and drama by specters of the dead, and steeped in the pessimistic view which traditional Buddhism took toward life in this world.

We must understand, however, that this "new" outlook was not just a sudden effusion of the human spirit, responding to changed conditions of life and breaking clearly with its past. On the contrary, certain attitudes most characteristic of Osaka in Saikaku's time quite plainly reflect its religious heritage as much as its new-found prosperity. Especially is this true of the theme treated in Saikaku's first great novels: the search for happiness in love. What at first sight seems no more than the universal preoccupation of man is soon seen to have a special quality, an extraordinary intensity akin to religious feeling. These townspeople went about making love as if it were a way of life in itself, as if, amidst the uncertainties of the world, love alone would endure. "In Love We Trust" might well have been the inscription on their coins, just coming into general circulation at that time.

There is here, no doubt, a defiant rejection of the traditional Buddhist view that all is dust and subject to corruption, that nothing escapes the universal law of change. But the protest bears a strong resemblance to one which had already come from within Buddhism itself, proclaiming salvation through loving faith in the Buddha Amida, whose abiding mercy and redemptive power alone could be relied upon to rescue men from the suffering of this world. Osaka itself had long been a stronghold of this new faith, and in the far more worldly atmosphere of the seventeenth century, as the people of that city looked increasingly to human love for happiness, it was still with the same sense of desperation and utter self-abandonment that was characteristic of Amida's devotees. Thus, Saikaku's heroines, forsaking the security of their homes and the "good things of life" to pursue some ill-fated affair, impress us less with their lusty relish for life than with their final unworldliness.

It is in this sense that we see a profound connection between the two seemingly disparate meanings of the word *ukiyo*—the Buddhists' "world of sadness" and the "floating world" of fashion and pleasure inhabited by Saikaku and his friends. They knew well enough that this new world was no more lasting than the old. Still, Saikaku, who sensed most keenly the vanity and pathos of existence in the Floating World, had not less but rather still more lively an appreciation of its ephemeral attractions and the wealth of experience which this new age opened to all. Certainly the pleasures of these townsmen were richer and more varied than any known before to ordinary Japanese, for success in commerce gave them the means to develop some of their other talents and the leisure to enjoy them. The warrior class, with all its past exploits, had nothing to compare with the entertainments of the city, and the Floating World lay before their wondering eyes like Cleopatra on her barge, luxuriating in an infinite variety of goods from exotic places, an endless life of salad days, and an elusive but unchangeable charm.

Wherever one found merchants and tradesmen in those times, there were sure to be signs of this new life described by Saikaku—busy markets, side lanes lined with little shops, the dignified establishments of money-changers, great warehouses, teahouses frequented by smartly dressed people, theatres, restaurants, bathhouses, brothels, and streets full of peddlers, panders, jugglers, freaks, and dancing shows. But in Saikaku's time no city was the equal of his own as a paradise for townspeople. Kyoto was still too conscious of its splendid past to live as Osaka did—for the present alone. The imperial court remained, making feeble pretense at its ancient elegance, and with it an aristocracy that did much to give Kyoto society its style and tone, even if it had the power to do little else. Meanwhile the warriors of the nation were establishing a new capital at Edo, now Tokyo, a fast-growing city with a political as well as commercial future. But under the watchful eyes of the shogunate, with a large warrior population to accommodate and with much of its effort devoted to the building of a new city, the townsmen of Edo were not at first so free to go their own way, to create a new life and make the most of it.

Osaka, perhaps, had less of a future in the political life of the country, but this fact served in part to stimulate its growth along independent lines. The city had once seemed to have such a future, and when the

Tokugawas took away their hope in it, the men of Osaka had another cause for resentment against the established order. Osaka had long been a city of commerical importance and was, along with the country at large, enjoying unprecedented prosperity when Toyotomi Hideyoshi chose it as his personal seat. There in 1583 he built the most formidable and elaborate fortified castle Japan had ever seen and planned extensive improvements in the city to make it the military and political as well as the economic heart of the nation. This it was indeed for the remaining fifteen years of his life. Then, not long after Hideyoshi's death, Tokugawa Ieyasu determined to erect his new capital at Edo, where he built a castle even more imposing than Hideyoshi's and started work on a metropolis that in time was to rival, and then outdo, Kyoto and Osaka in importance.

In the meantime Osaka remained a source of wealth and power to Hideyoshi's heir, Hideyori, who strengthened himself there by recruiting thousands of warriors, the lordless *ronin,* dispossessed by Ieyasu after their defeat by him at Sekigahara. Then in 1615 Hideyori too was brought low by Ieyasu, after a year of savage fighting, which featured the new destructive power of Western firearms and laid waste much of the city. Still the men of Osaka had spirit and strength enough to undertake its reconstruction on a grander scale than before. They had the encouragement of

Matsudaira Tadaaki, a hereditary vassal of the Tokugawas who was entrusted with the rule of this key
domain after Hideyori's fall. He reorganized its ad-
ministrative structure, setting up local councils of elders
drawn from the propertied and moneyed men of the
city. Above them he placed another council, similarly
chosen, which determined policy for the city as a whole
and gave it a significant measure of self-rule.

A prominent member of this city council was Yasui
Doton, who through his success in business and service
to the city became a model of those virtues on which
the leading citizens of Osaka prided themselves. As
chairman of the committee on public improvements,
he did much toward the planning of the new city;
the construction of streets, bridges, and canals, which
promoted business; and the building of theatres, which
brought entertainment to his fellow citizens on a scale
unknown before. Yasui and other wealthy men contributed heavily to these projects. Some contribution
was even made by the Tokugawa Shogunate: Iemitsu
exempted the city from land taxes for one year and
donated over four hundred pounds of silver to finance
the work of bridgebuilding. But this was a small
investment beside that which the shogunate was putting into Edo, and to the citizens of Osaka must go
most of the credit for the improvements made in their
own city. Of the bridges alone more than thirty were
built with funds raised by local subscription; eleven

were built with the assistance of their military masters. We will find Saikaku speaking of the Dotom-bori, a canal named after Yasui Doton, who financed its construction, and of the Yodoya-bashi, a bridge named for the same reason after the wealthiest man of the day.

This Yodoya, a rice merchant, was as much a symbol of his time as Yasui. His fortune is said to have included 21 solid-gold hens, with 10 chickens; 14 solid-gold macaws; 15 solid-gold sparrows; 51 solid-gold-and-silver doves; innumerable precious stones; 150 pounds of quicksilver; more than 700 swords; over 17,000 rolls of velvet, silk, and brocade; 480 carpets; 50 pairs of gold screens; 96 crystal sliding doors; a solid-gold checkerboard three inches thick; 3,500,000 *ryo* in gold coin (roughly 146,000 pounds troy); 14,000,000 *ryo* in silver (roughly 583,000 pounds troy); 550,000 copper coins; about 750 Chinese paintings; 540 mansions, houses, and warehouses; and 250 farms and fields. Most of this wealth had been accumulated by two generations of Yodoyas, after the family residence had been converted into an open market where feudal lords could exchange their rice for money, then just coming into general use. Thus the fortune was made at the expense of the lords themselves, who had little talent for business. From this we may judge that it was not in the interests of economy alone that the shogun censured Yodoya for his extravagant ways, and finally confiscated his wealth entirely. Yodoya was dangerous, not just as a bad example for the shogun's subjects, but also as a rival potentate, an upstart who bled his betters in order to create a strange new empire.

From the account of a Dutch emissary, Engelbert Kaempfer, who visited Osaka in 1692, we may see what sort of city was created by men like Yodoya and Yasui. "Osacca," he wrote in his *History of Japan,* "is extremely populous, and if we believe what the boasting Japanese tell us, can raise an army of 80,000 men, only from among its inhabitants. It is the best trading town in Japan, being extraordinarily well-situated for carrying on commerce both by land and water. This is the reason why it is well-inhabited by rich merchants, artificers and manufacturers. Victuals are cheap at Osacca, notwithstanding the city is so well-peopled. Even what tends to promote luxury, and to gratify all sensual pleasures, may be had at as easy a rate as anywhere. For this reason the Japanese call Osacca the universal theatre of pleasures and diversions. Plays are to be seen daily both in public and private houses. Mountebanks, juglers who can show some artful tricks, and all rary-shew people, who have either some uncommon or monstrous animal to show, or animals taught to play tricks, resort thither from all parts of the Empire, being sure to get a better penny here than anywhere else. Of this one instance will suffice. Some years ago, our East India Company sent over from Batavia a Casuar (a large East India bird who would swallow stones and

hot coals) as a present to the Emperor. This bird having
had the ill-luck not to please our rigid censors, the
Governors of Nagasaki, to whom it belongs to deter-
mine what presents might be acceptable to the Emperor,
and we having been thereupon ordered to send him
back to Batavia, a rich Japanese and lover of these
curiosities assured us, that if he could have obtained
leave to buy him, he would have willingly given a
thousand thails for him, as being sure within a year's
time to get double that money only by shewing him in
Osacca."

Ihara Saikaku was born in this city in 1642. Nothing
is known about his early life and very little even about
his later years. His wife died young, leaving him with
a blind daughter, who also died within a few years. It
is said that Saikaku's grief led him to place his affairs
in the hands of an assistant, but instead of retiring to
some religious sanctuary as might have been expected,
he devoted himself to travel and writing. We may
judge from his novels that his journeying about Japan
in those early years provided him with a rich store
of information from which to draw for local color and
charming incidents. His knowledge of places, peoples,
and things was, for a novelist, probably equal to that
which the famous actor Sakata Tojuro expected of his
own profession: "The art of an actor is like a beggar's
bag and must contain everything, whether it is important or not. If there is anything not wanted for

immediate use, keep it for a future occasion. An actor should even learn how to pick pockets."

Saikaku first won literary recognition as the leading disciple of Soin, a writer of *haikai* (seventeen-syllable epigrammatic verses linked into long poems) who headed the liberal Danrin school of poetry. As the chief exponent of this school in Osaka, Saikaku was influential in the movement to free poetry from rigid adherence to conventional forms, to enlarge the scope of its subject matter, and to have it read in a natural style. His predilection for commonplace themes, drawn from the daily life of the people, won for him the contempt of the famous poet Basho, who found Saikaku's verse vulgar and uninspired, but it made him enormously popular for a time in Osaka. Saikaku was especially famous for his marathon poetry-performances before assembled friends and admirers. At the age of thirty-six he is said to have composed sixteen hundred *haikai* in a single performance, a feat which put this kind of versification for the first time into mass production on a competitive basis. Three years later his record output for a single day went up to three thousand, and finally, at the age of forty-three, Saikaku put on a day-and-night exhibition which resulted, it was claimed, in the composing of 23,500 of these versified epigrams. On such occasions Saikaku had judges standing by to count and record the *haikai* he composed. Moreover, the nickname which he acquired,

Ni-man Okina ('Twenty-thousand Old Master), suggests that people in his own time thought him capable
of this spectacular accomplishment.

These public orgies seem to have exhausted for the
moment Saikaku's appetite for expression in the limited, if not inflexible, *haikai* form. He turned now to
writing fiction, finding this medium perhaps better
suited to the development of his subject matter because
it permitted a far wider range of expression than did
epigrammatic verse. In these same years Saikaku also
tried his hand at playwriting and at recording his ob-
servations on theatre people of his time, especially the
personal charms of young actors and amusing details
of their private lives. But it was the novel which gave
full scope both to his rich poetical imagination and to
his talent for realistic observation of the life of his time.

Saikaku's first novel, *Koshoku ichidai otoko* (A
Man Who Loved Love), tells of a man who roamed
around the country, working at all sorts of trades, and
making love to thousands of women and hundreds of
young boys. It is considered by many Japanese as his
most realistic novel, while *Five Women Who Loved
Love* is thought more imaginative and poetic. The
former is likened to *The Tale of Genji,* some even
saying that Saikaku used *Genji* for his model. But
whatever Saikaku may have owed to earlier literature,
including tales of the Floating World (*ukiyo-zoshi*),
which were popular in his own time, he did much to

create a type of literature new to Japan, and at the same time to give the common people an equivalent for the *Genji* in terms of their own experience. The hero of his first novel was as handsome and accomplished a lover as Prince Genji, but instead of luxuriating in the magnificent surroundings of the court, he found his pleasure where Saikaku's readers looked for theirs—in teahouses, brothels, bathhouses, theatres, and the homes of commoners. The heroes and heroines of his other romances, including *Five Women Who Loved Love,* bear much less resemblance to people in Murasaki's *Tale of Genji,* yet we often find them aping the latter. When some young bucks of Kyoto spend an evening at a teahouse, passing judgment on the beauty and dress of the girls who come by, they do in their own way what Genji and his friends did in discussing the virtues and desirability of various court ladies. When a girl comes upon her sleeping lover, she finds his body perfumed with a scent named after Genji's only son. Even the brothel women have "Genji names," taken from those given to the emperor's ladies. Nevertheless, there is one respect at least in which this Floating World differed strikingly from the society of Genji—it was more open and varied. Where Murasaki and her circle had made the court their whole world, Saikaku and his friends thought to make the whole world their court.

Not all of Saikaku's novels concern the love of men

and women, as do the two already mentioned. But much of what he had to say in other novels is suggested in these. There is, for instance, the matter of men who loved men, which became the subject of a later series, the *Nanshoku okagami* (Mirror of Manly Love). By Saikaku's time pederasty had become fairly widespread in Japan. Its origins have been traced back to the Heian period (ninth and tenth centuries A.D.), when the growth of monasticism made it common among Buddhist monks, who were forbidden the company of women. A homosexual relationship developed between master and disciple, the older monk acting as teacher and guardian in return for the love and devotion of his younger partner. During medieval times this custom spread to the warrior class, where it fitted into the order of feudal loyalties. Obedience and service on the part of a younger man were exchanged for the favor and protection of an older one, and their love was solemnized by an oath of faithfulness to each other for life. In the early Tokugawa period prohibitions were placed on this practice by the shogunate, but it continued to flourish in places where the latter's influence was too weak to enforce compliance, some of them places where an individualistic and warlike tradition was still strong and men scorned the love of women as effeminate. Satsuma was one of these, and the last of Saikaku's five women had to win her Satsuma man away from the love of young boys.

It is perhaps as a reward for her success that Saikaku lets this girl, alone among his heroines, enjoy a happy ending to her story. The others all die, commit suicide, or enter a nunnery, but she and her lover are brought back in triumph for a marriage in her father's home, where there is wealth enough for her mate to dream, still, of buying up all the theatres in Japan with all their pretty male actors. It is a story suggestive of many things: for one, that in Saikaku's time the theatre was a stronghold of homosexual love. Saikaku speaks also of Buddhist temples and Shinto shrines as favorite haunts of homosexuals, but the all-male theatre probably did more than any other institution to promote the love of men for men and make it seem less unnatural to society as a whole. When women were barred from the acting profession for having combined it with another, less seemly calling, handsome young men in women's roles became the idols of both sexes in their audience.

What drew Saikaku to this subject was not simply the realistic writer's desire to mirror his society or describe impartially the varieties of love practiced in his time. Such a cool detachment would have been quite spurious with him, for Saikaku's sharp objectivity implied no dulling of his human sympathies or his moral sensibility. Nor could he delve into the inmost secrets of human life only to expose them to ridicule or snickering prurience. Saikaku was obviously fascinated by the variety and complexity of human love, but, retaining always a sense of its intrinsic dignity, of love in its most exalted form as leading to self-denial rather than self-gratification, he is both a discriminating and compassionate judge of his fellow men. Thus it is not the sensual aspects of homosexual love that he takes up, but the theme of heroic devotion or base disloyalty.

There is another kind of love which, as we might expect, figures even more prominently in Saikaku's writings: the love of money—of riches generally, but in particular of coined money, which was a new object of love in those days and worth writing about in itself. In the *Eitai-gura* (Treasury for the Ages) he says: "It is not plum, cherry, pine, and maple trees that people desire most around their houses, but gold, silver, rice, and hard cash." The whole book is devoted to showing how men went about satisfying this desire, as is another, *Seken mune-zanyo* (The Calculating World). While *Five Women Who Loved Love* is written mostly about people enjoying the pleasures of an already-earned wealth, two of its heroes have to think about acquiring it, and we know from them something of what Saikaku thought was essential to the making of money: frugality, persistence, a ready mind for figures, mastery of the abacus, a pleasant manner, honesty, and imagination.

Most of these virtues had not been made much of

before. The businessmen's creed was new and Saikaku was its first publicist in Japan. It was developed largely by a class of merchants and moneylenders, called *kami-gata-mono,* who had become active in the Kyoto-Osaka region during the sixteenth and seventeenth centuries. These were the men whose resourcefulness, we are told, created the merchant guilds (*za*) in Japan, the free ports, free markets, the use of gold and silver as legal tender, paper money, and bills of exchange. Among them were some who had gone abroad in search of fortune and, when ordered home by the shogunate, had brought back to the port cities a new sense of freedom, an acquaintance with other ways of life, and especially a better knowledge of trade and money-handling. From them, we may imagine, the people of these cities learned to look outward and ahead, rather than inward and back as did the framers of the Tokugawa seclusion policy.

To them also Saikaku must have owed much of his curiosity about the world and his taste for the exotic. Long ago exoticism had captured the Japanese mind, during the first flush of Buddhism and Chinese learning, but it later languished in a medieval dungeon of introspection and antiquarianism. Saikaku was one of those who brought it back to life in literature. He was fascinated both by the great variety of wealth in his own country and the innumerable treasures of foreign lands. The known world was, indeed, hardly

enough to satisfy his thirst for the exotic. He followed
the map to its limits when he had a dissolute company
of pleasure seekers play "naked islanders such as are
mentioned on maps of the world." And when he
came to the end of this book, to the treasure of a man
from the Ryukyus, Saikaku could not be happy with
such precious gifts as the silks of China and jewels
and incense wood of the Indies. He had to have
wonders from a Taoist paradise and the palaces of the
gods.

Saikaku's enormous appetite for the wonders of the
world earned for him the additional nickname Oranda
Saikaku (Holland Saikaku). This did not mean, so
far as we know, that Saikaku had any special acquaintance with the Dutch, who were then the only foreign
traders allowed into Japan, or that he was in fact a
student of Dutch learning. Rather it meant that people thought him unconventional enough to have a taste
for things foreign or strange. The epithet was probably
first applied contemptuously by persons who wanted
to brand him as a nonconformist.

The heart of his nonconformity was not, however,
his exoticism. It was his adherence to the way of the
townspeople and his belief that, in the cities at least,
successful businessmen were the real aristocrats, while
high birth and military prowess counted for little. This
belief is expressed in one way by what he says in the
Treasury for the Ages: "It makes no difference whether

a man is of humble birth or of fine lineage. The geneologies of townspeople are written in dollars and cents. A man who traces his ancestry to Fujiwara Kamatari [a noble of the highest court rank] but who lives impoverished in the city will be worse off than one who leads a monkey through the streets to earn his living." And the same belief is expressed in another way in Saikaku's stories of the warrior class, such as the *Buke-giri monogatari* (The Warrior's Sense of Duty). Though ostensibly written to popularize the way of the warrior, these stories leave a final impression of the warrior class as useless, misguided, and worthy of sympathy rather than admiration.

Still, it is with the individual that Saikaku is ultimately concerned, not the substitution of one type of class-thinking for another. Even among the townspeople, whom Saikaku loves, there is no general title to admiration and success. The virtues of industry and frugality can easily be corrupted to make men overscrupulous and stingy, as in the example of Moemon, who economized on his coat sleeves, would not buy a hat when he came of age to wear one, and slept with an abacus under his pillow to keep track of the money he made in dreams. But, somewhat like Gengobei, Moemon is one minute a ridiculous clerk and the next a daring hero who runs off with the most beautiful lady in town. Saikaku is as loath to confine his people in rigid characterization as in tight social classes.

They are consistent only in their need for happiness and their weakness in pursuit of it. The reader must be quick if he is to follow the unpredictable course of human behavior and learn its secrets.

Saikaku is not one to accommodate a Western reader's taste for consistency in other matters, either. Time and place mean nothing to him except as they serve to create a mood. He will stop the sun in its course if he needs a sunset at the beginning and end of a picnic; he rushes the seasons to get the appropriate atmosphere for a certain scene. Sometimes people seem to be everywhere at once, and Gengobei, as a street-singer, impersonates himself as if he had already become a legend. One woman is successfully seduced while asleep, and a man spends the night with a young friend, waking to find it all a dream and his friend long since dead. Nothing is too implausible for the logic of mood and emotion.

But his readers would probably not have held Saikaku accountable for such contradictions and inconsistencies. Many of Saikaku's characters were already known in popular drama and song, and he was obliged to respect in some degree the associations people had with their names, to make them do some of the things for which they were already celebrated. It did not matter whether these things fitted poorly into the rest of the story; the thrill of identifying an old hero or favorite actor was enough. We should also bear in mind that Saikaku wrote *Five Women Who Loved Love* in some haste. It was the second of five books published within a period of only twelve months, and he probably spent little time trying to straighten out inconsistencies.

There is another set of conventions which the Western reader may be surprised, this time pleasantly, to find disregarded by Saikaku: that deriving from what is considered the Japanese' overdeveloped sense of politeness and discretion. Their absence in Saikaku may be due in part to the fact that his stories move too swiftly to allow for lengthy circumlocutions or polite explanations of what people do. Saikaku is customarily forthright himself—a quality which he probably shared with most other townsmen of the time—and his characters are generally direct in going about what they wish to do. In *Five Women Who Loved Love* this is most noticeable in the impetuosity of his heroines. They do not wait to be wooed by the men of their choice or stand by timidly while customary procedures decide their fate. In each case the heroine makes the advances, forces the issue, decides what must be done in a crisis. And when her impetuosity leads to ruin for herself and her lover, as most often happens, it is the heroine again whose unchastened spirit dominates the final scene at the execution ground.

For Saikaku this boldness is what makes a woman great, more than her beauty. Nevertheless, his heroines are weak as well as strong, and he does not spare them the consequences of their weakness—in most cases, death. This ultimate retribution is not brought about merely to satisfy conventional morality, nor is it, on the other hand, held up as the final injustice done by society to a girl more sinned against than sinning. Death may be too extreme a penalty to pay for such offenses, but offenses they are nonetheless. To Saikaku the moral order is as hard and inescapable a fact as human passion.

In this respect, despite the reputation he was later to acquire as a skillful teller of erotic tales, Saikaku is a keener and more effective judge of human foibles than many a writer whose purpose is more obviously moralistic. Saikaku never appears as the doctrinaire proponent of a particular moral philosophy. He does not, like the playwright Chikamatsu, lend his talents to the movement which popularized Confucian ethics in the seventeenth and eighteenth centuries. The moral law prevails, but Saikaku cannot pretend that his heroines are easily reconciled to it. His five women remain wholly themselves—temperamental, volatile, passionate, unpredictable. Nothing is done to redeem them at the last, as Chikamatsu does with his Confucian puppets, by showing them to be good and reasonable people after all, whose sins are more the fault of circumstances than their own, and who with Chikamatsu's approval can petulantly protest love for parents they have disgraced or loyal obedience to masters they have betrayed.

In Chikamatsu's "Almanac of Love" (translated by A. Miyamori in *Masterpieces of Chikamatsu,* London, 1926), which takes up the same theme as the third of our stories here, Osan is remorseful, not for what she has done to herself, but for having brought shame to her father and for having implicated the guiltless Tama as go-between in her adulterous affair; Moemon is not, we are asked to believe, concerned for his own life, but wishes only another chance to prove himself a loyal servant of the man he made a cuckold; and Osan's father, who must be both a staunch upholder of the law and a loving father to Osan, tells her that he cannot give her money with which to escape the law, but that he will drop some money on the floor and there is nothing to prevent her picking it up. In the end goodness and order prevail, every Confucian virtue is accounted for, and a compromise is worked out whereby no one dies but the guiltless Tama, whose head is sacrificed in her father's frantic attempt to have justice done and still save the guilty!

In Saikaku's story, Osan's only regrets are for herself. Her elopement with Moemon, with its elaborate hoax to make people think them dead, proves a miserable affair; she is a wretched fugitive, without the strength for flight through the wilderness, and is sustained only by Moemon's promise of an early chance

to go to bed together. Moemon returns to the scene
of his crime, not in the hope of redemption, but because
he must hear what people are saying about him and
because he is homesick for Kyoto after weeks of plea-
sureless life in the country. In the end both must
die—a poignant death, because they are not ordinary
lovers and everyone pities their frailty—while the war
between passion and prudence goes on. Reason wins
no false victory; it succeeds only in showing men as
they are, at their best and at their worst.

But with Saikaku the consequence of sin is not
always death. Sometimes there is an alternative in the
Buddhist monastery, where a ruined lover can pray
for the soul of his beloved and hope to be reunited
with her in paradise. The monastery is, in fact, such
a ready alternative that it seems to have become simply
a place for escaping from the world. It is not a place
one goes to escape oneself. This is because the lover
remains a lover, and goes to the monastery in order to
remain faithful to his love. There is little consciousness of personal sin, no estrangement from God or
repentance. In death the lovers are defiant because
the world is against them; in the monastery they are
resigned, confident that they will have ultimate victory
over the world.

What Saikaku's characters are more conscious of than
personal sin, as we know it, is a sort of Original and
Perpetual Sin, known as karma or *inga,* the chain of

moral causation which conditions one's life in accordance with one's past actions. Strictly speaking, it was possible by one's actions to lighten the burden or add to it, as one chose. In practice, however, the overcoming of sin and the acquisition of merit depended upon the individual's capacity for enlightened conduct. It came to be recognized that few men were sufficiently enlightened to cope with the weight of karma accumulated through innumerable previous existences. Thereupon a savior appeared in the Buddha Amida, who had vowed that his great accumulation of merit should be applied to the salvation of all men, so that they might, without any merit of their own, share with him the pleasures of the Western Paradise. Redemption was then free for the asking, not a reward for good conduct in this life.

For this reason, when Saikaku's lovers speak of their misfortunes as due to karma, to them it is almost the equivalent of Fate because they feel helpless under its crushing weight. In some cases there is a further complication arising from a Buddhist superstition called *shushin:* a curse which falls upon someone who refuses to gratify the love of another. Thus, unequal to karma, threatened perhaps by the curse of a disappointed lover, and feeling desperately the urge to seize a brief moment of bliss in this dreary world, Saikaku's five women plunge headlong and headstrong into love, into death, into the cloister—with the name of Amida on their lips, and in their souls a faith that salvation depends on the Buddha's love, not upon what they do themselves.

We may believe that they are real people as well as Saikaku's creatures. We know enough about the life of his society and the celebrated cases of ill-fated lovers to recognize them as people of his own time. And yet what Saikaku has to tell us about them takes a form much different from the realistic novel to which we are accustomed. This is a work of poetry and imagination, not simply of skilled observation. Saikaku is no social scientist. He is indeed a sorcerer, whose powers are unexpectedly used to bring all of life out into the light of day, after his friends, in their search of fugitive pleasures, have turned day into "a kingdom of eternal night."

W. T. DE B.

Book One

The Story of Seijuro in Himeji

1. Darkness is the time for love; love makes night of day

In spring the treasure ships lay, with waves their pillows, on a quiet sea before the bustling harbor of Murotsu. In this town lived a saké-brewing merchant, Izumi Seizaemon, whose house prospered and lacked nothing. He was blessed, moreover, with a son named Seijuro, whose natural beauty and grace exceeded even that attributed in pictures to the hero of olden days, Narihira.

Handsome as he was and graced with manners pleasing to women, Seijuro had been familiar with the ways of love since late in his thirteenth year. In Murotsu the women of pleasure numbered eighty-seven, and there was none he had not known. The vows of love written during his affairs might have been bound into a thousand packets, and the fingernails his mistresses had sent as pledges of their devotion were more than a ditty box could hold. There had been sent, too, as tokens of love, enough black locks to make a heavy rope of hair, entwining even the most jealous of women. Each day brought a small mountain of love letters, and gift garments of silk bearing their professional crests, which he tossed aside unworn into a heap —clothing enough to appease forever the greed of the old woman at the River of Three Crossings,[1] were she to see them; and garments of such quality as to prove too precious for all the secondhand dealers at the Korean Bridge.[2] Seijuro stuffed them away and put a sign before his door: "Treasure House of the Floating World."

But where in the world can such idle foolishness prosper? Those who saw what was going on grieved and said: "Before long you will find yourself disinherited." Still, it is hard to break away from a life of pleasure, and about that time Seijuro fell in love with a courtesan named Minakawa, so desperately and with such uncommon passion that he was oblivious to the gossip of society and the disparaging remarks of individuals.

One day he burned lanterns, more wastefully than on a moonlit night, in the house of assignation he

[1] *Sanzu-gawa*—in hell, where she stood guard and deprived sinners of their clothes.
[2] In Osaka.

frequented. Shutting the doors and blinds to cut out the light, he created a place for constant entertainment, a kingdom of eternal night. He gathered fools to amuse his party with imitations of bats crying or of watchmen clacking their wooden clappers. Procuresses chanted Buddhist prayers while making offerings of tea for passers-by and performed a mock mass, saying it was for the repose of Kyugoro, one of the company who was very much alive. Instead of funeral incense they burned toothpicks and by the flickering light exhausted their repertoire of things commonly done at night. Finally, under the pretext of playing "naked islanders," such as one sees mentioned on maps of the world, the courtesans were made to disrobe in spite of their unwillingness. Among those who blushed at being seen naked was a young novice named Yoshizaki, on whose hip was discovered a white blemish which she had kept concealed. Disenchanted at the sight of this splotch, the assembled guests ridiculed her by saying "A veritable Venus!" and jokingly bowed in homage. Looking then at the other women, they realized there was none without some blemish to her beauty, and gradually the guests lost interest in even these amusements.

Just then Seijuro's father, bursting into the house in a great rage, caught the company unprepared, as when a sudden gust of wind strikes before the house-holder can put anything away.

"Forgive me," Seijuro pleaded. "I will carry this foolishness no further."

But his father listened to none of these apologies. "Get out of here and begone with you," he commanded. Then, brusquely taking leave of the company, he quickly departed.

Greatly distressed, Minakawa and the other women broke into tears. But Jisuke of the Black Night, one of the entertainers, was not at all abashed.

"Even a naked man," he said, referring to the disinherited Seijuro, "is worth something. With only a loincloth one can still make out in this world. Don't let it discourage you, Seijuro." Thus amidst the despair he found something gay to offer the company as an appetizer for more wine, and drinking, they soon forgot the unpleasantness.

Not so the proprietors of the pleasure house, however, whose hospitality soon showed signs of cooling. When the guests clapped for service there was no answer. Nor was there any soup when the time for it came. Tea was brought in by hand, two cups at a time, instead of on the usual tray. And the servants, as they left, turned down the lampwicks to dim the room. Finally, one by one, the courtesans were called away.

Alas, fickleness is the rule in pleasure houses, and human kindness is measured out in small change.

Minakawa, grieved to the bottom of her heart, stayed behind when the others had gone and sank into tears.

Seijuro could only say, "It's heart-rending," and thought to himself that he would take his own life, if only Minakawa would not insist on joining him.

She guessed what he had in mind, and said: "You are thinking of taking your life. Alas, how foolish! For, however much I should like to say, 'Take me with you,' I still have attachments in this world and cannot. In my sort of work one's heart belongs first to this man, then to that. Let us simply call our affair a thing of the past." So saying, she rose and left him.

Crushed by these unexpected words, Seijuro abandoned his plan of suicide. "How fickle these whores are! Ready any time to cast away old lovers."

But as he rose in tears to leave, Minakawa came back clothed in garments of white, ready now to die, and clung desperately to him. "How can you live? Where will you go? Oh, now is the time to end it all!" she cried, pulling out a pair of knives.

Seijuro was almost speechless with delight to find his lover faithful after all. But the brothel people, seeing what was going on, drew them apart and led

"...Oh, now is the time to end it all!" she cried, pulling out a pair of knives. Seijuro was almost speechless with delight to find his lover faithful after all. But the brothel people ... drew them apart....

Minakawa back to her master. Seijuro they took to the Eiko-in, his family temple, where he might start anew and perhaps someday restore himself in his father's good graces. Thus at eighteen his only prospect was to take up holy orders. How pitiful indeed!

2. *Letters in the seams of a sash*

"Something terrible just happened! Get a doctor, get some smelling salts!" someone cried.

There was a great commotion. "What is it?"

"Minakawa—suicide!" was the answer. In their distress no one could do anything to save her, and soon her heart beat its last. Such is the sad way of this world.

For more than ten days the news was kept from Seijuro. When he heard it he was disconsolate to think of living on alone after Minakawa had died. But because of a note his mother wrote him, he decided for her sake to carry on his unhappy existence. Stealing out of the Eiko-in, he quietly departed for the town of Himeji to seek the help of some friends there.

These friends knew he came from a good family, and they treated him well. After some time had passed it was learned that the proprieter of the Tajima-ya was looking for an assistant to take charge of his shop, and Seijuro was promised a bright future if he would enter the business. So it was arranged, through the good offices of the man with whom he was staying, for Seijuro to undertake his first apprenticeship.

He did well. His gentlemanly breeding, his kindliness and intelligence, made him well liked. He plunged into his work wholeheartedly and, having no longer an appetite for love, concerned himself solely with the improvement of his character. His master left all business affairs to Seijuro, who conducted them so profitably that he became more and more indispensable to Master Kyuemon's plans for the future.

Kyuemon, however, had a sister named Onatsu, who, though romantically inclined, at sixteen had not yet become involved in any serious love affairs. Among country girls certainly, and perhaps among the modest daughters of Kyoto, her loveliness could not be equaled. People even said that Onatsu surpassed in beauty the former queen of courtesans in Shimabara, the one whose crest displayed the raised wings of a butterfly. We need not mention here the many ways in which she was thought to resemble her. Suffice it to say, Onatsu had the makings of a superb lover.

It happened that Seijuro one day went to the chief

maidservant, Kame, and handed her an everyday silk sash of dragon design. "This is a little too wide to suit me. Won't you fix it?" he asked.

Later, as she pulled apart the seams, Kame discovered some old letters hidden inside and, grabbing them up, read one after another. There were fourteen or fifteen in all, each addressed to Seijuro under the nickname "Mr. Kiyo." The signatures differed, however: Hanacho, Ukifune, Kodayu, Akashi, Unoha, Chikuzen, Senju, Ichi-no-jo, Koyoshi, Choshu, Matsuyama, Kozaemon, Dewa, and Miyoshi—all names of prostitutes in Murotsu. Every one of them revealed a deep attachment to Seijuro, a selfless love expressed with remarkable sincerity. In none of the letters could be found the artificiality or lewd suggestiveness to which women of this profession are often addicted. They wrote freely and straightforwardly, and if one could judge from their letters alone, these prostitutes were not at all to be despised.

Seeing the letters, a woman would be inclined to think that Seijuro had received some benefit from his wild days in the gay world of pleasure, a benefit, perhaps, concealed from all but those who knew him intimately enough to learn what secret skills he had acquired through long experience. At any rate, this thought occured one day to Onatsu.

From then on, from morn till night, her heart was consumed with desire for Seijuro. It was as if her soul had departed from her body and lodged itself in the breast of her beloved. She spoke as one in a dream. To her obsessed senses the flowers of spring were obscured in darkness, and the moon of autumn seemed no different from daylight. She could not see the whiteness of the winter snow at dawn, nor hear the cuckoo of a summer evening. Indeed, she was unaware of the season, whether it was New Year's or time for the midsummer festival of O-Bon.[3] Finally she forgot herself completely. Her eyes blushed openly with love, and her passion was laid bare by the words she spoke.

After all, the other maids thought, this happens to everyone some time. They pitied Onatsu deeply and wished they could help her, but each had come to feel her own love for Seijuro. The seamstress had sent him a love note written in blood drawn by her own needle. The chief maidservant, unable to write, had asked a man to prepare a letter for her, though his masculine hand betrayed itself. Then she slipped it into Seijuro's sleeve. The chambermaid took tea into the shop for him when there was no need for it. Under the pretense of letting Baby see Seijuro, the nurse approached

[3] Festival in August for the returning spirits of the dead.

...*as she pulled apart the seams, Kame discovered some old
letters hidden inside and, grabbing them up, read one
after another. There were fourteen or fifteen
in all, each addressed to Seijuro....*

*Under the pretense of letting Baby see Seijuro, the nurse . . .
placed her ward in his arms, whereupon Baby immediately wet Seijuro's lap. "It's time you too
had a little one like this," she said. . . .*

him and placed her ward in his arms, whereupon Baby immediately wet Seijuro's lap.

"It's time you too had a little one like this," she said. "I once had a pretty child myself, before I came here as a nurse. But my man was a good-for-nothing. He went off to Kumamoto in Higo Province and has some sort of apprenticeship there, according to what I hear. When we broke up housekeeping I got separation papers and am free again now. Of course," she added, lisping on in a monologue of coy self-deprecia-tion, "I was born a bit plump; my mouth is small and my hair is somewhat kinky. . . ."

The waitresses too, when ladling out fish stew to the hired men at mealtime, were always scrupulously care-ful to save the choice parts for Seijuro.

For his part Seijuro was pleased, but not entirely so, by the advances made toward him from all sides. They interfered with his work and kept him ceaselessly busy answering all the letters. Eventually he found it very tiresome, for even his dreams were disturbed and he slept with open eyes.

Still Onatsu persisted and found the means to send him one passionate letter after another, until finally Seijuro yielded his heart to her. But the house was full of busy eyes. The lovers found no opportunity to enjoy each other's company, and while their passion smouldered under such restraint their bodies grew gaunt, stretched upon the rack of love. Thus the days passed without relief, until at last it seemed delightful enough to them simply to hear each other's voices once in a while.

But in life lies the seed of all things. The lovers felt that, living on, they might someday be brought together, as the wind by chance bends two blades of grass. If only it were not for Onatsu's sister-in-law, who never failed to lock the door which stood across the passageway between them!

"Be careful about fire," she would call, and then shut the door with a rattle-and-clap more dreadful than thunder to the ears of the wakeful lovers.

3. *A lion dances to the beat of a drum*

When cherry trees bloom at Onoe[4] men's wives bloom too with a new pride in their appearance, and pretty girls go strolling with their proud mothers, not so much to see the spring blossoms as to be seen themselves. That is the way people are these days; at least

[4] A place in Harima famed for its cherry blossoms.

that is the way with women. They are witches who could enchant even the wizard fox of Himeji Castle.

One spring day the women of the Tajima-ya household decided to go to the woods for a picnic, to which the ladies were borne in litters followed by Seijuro, the supervisor of the affair. The far-famed pines of Takasago and Sone were in early-spring verdure, and there was no sight to equal the loveliness of the sandy beach. To see the boys of the village clearing the dead leaves with rakes and hunting eagerly for mushroom buttons, reed-flowers, and violets was a rare treat for the ladies, who each expressed an urge to do the same. Soon they picked out a spot barely overgrown with young grass, and there spread out their flower-mats and carpets.

The sea and fields were still, as the setting sun vied with the resplendent red garments of our ladies for favor in the eyes of all. In the company of ladies dressed in such brilliant colors, the wisteria and yellow rose went unnoticed by the throng of other picnickers who had come to see the flowers but now peered instead into our party's curtained enclosure and were charmed by the sight of pretty maids inside. Forgetting the hour for departure, forgetting everything, these picknickers opened up casks of wine and proclaimed drunkenness man's greatest delight. Thus,

with the enticing sight of the ladies as an appetizer
for the afternoon's revels, they enjoyed themselves to
their hearts' content.

Seijuro was the only man within his party's curtained enclosure, but the girls drank their full share
of wine, and outside the litter-bearers helped themselves to large cups until they fell into a drunken sleep,
snoring deeply and dreaming blissfully of themselves
as butterflies fluttering at will over the broad fields. At
this juncture the other people in the grove suddenly
gathered round to watch a passing band of entertainers
with a big drum and lion dancers. The troupe passed
from one picnic place to another, as the dancers put
on a skillful show in imitation of the lion shaking and
waving its head. The girls were fascinated by it and
abandoned all their other amusements to crowd
around, applaud, and cry for encore after encore, lest
the entertainment stop too soon. So the troupe stayed
there, in that one spot, to run through its whole repertoire of pretty songs.

Onatsu, however, was not among the onlookers.
She seemed to be indisposed with a painful toothache
and remained alone behind the curtains, resting on her
elbow, her sash undone, in complete disarray. Screen-
ing her from view was a pile of extra garments, behind
which she pretended to snore as if asleep.

...the dancers put on a skillful show in imitation of the lion shaking and waving its head.... Who would think of this as a good chance to make love, when there could be only a brief moment for consummation?...

Who would think of this as a good chance to make love, when there could be only a brief moment for consummation? None but the most determined and accomplished of lovers—certainly no city girl would ever dream of it. But Seijuro, quickly noticing that Onatsu was left alone, went around the back way, through a luxuriant growth of pines, to find his lover beckoning to him. Caring little that Onatsu's hairdress might become disarranged, the two clasped each other tight, breathing heavily, and their hearts beating fast. Fearful, however, of being discovered by Onatsu's sister-in-law, they kept their eyes on the spectators beyond the tent.

It was not until they arose that they noticed behind them a woodcutter, who had come up and laid down his load of wood. Holding his sickle in one hand and moving his underpants about with the other, he stood there watching the couple intently, amazed and amused. Truly this was a case of "hiding one's head and leaving the tail unguarded."

When Seijuro finally left the curtained enclosure, the performers put a stop to the entertainment outside, although some of the best parts of it remained unplayed. Many of the picnickers were disappointed by this sudden halting of the show, but already a thick mist was settling in and the evening sun was falling

fast, so they got their things together and started back
to Himeji. Onatsu did not seem to be aware of the
mess that had been made of her kimono in the back.

Seijuro, following them, was profuse in his thanks
to the company of lion dancers. "I am indeed indebted
to you for your services today."

Think of it! This passing show had actually been
arranged in advance, the clever strategem of a desperate
lover. Perhaps even the wise gods knew nothing of
his secret. And the others, especially that know-it-all
wife of Onatsu's brother—what chance had they of
knowing?

4. *The fellow who left the mailbag behind at an inn*

Now that the affair had been successfully launched,
Seijuro hurried it to its destination and eloped with
Onatsu, the two hastening to reach the port of Shika-
mazu by dusk.

"If we go together to Osaka or Kyoto, I know that
we would be happy there, even if it meant having to
live in poverty for many years." Thus Seijuro had
resolved and, having made the necessary preparations,

they were soon dressed in traveling clothes and standing in a shabby waiting room on the ferry pier. Waiting with them were some pilgrims bound for the Great Shrine at Ise, a hardware merchant from Osaka, a dealer in lacquer from Nara, a Buddhist priest from the monastery at Daigo, a tea-set seller from Takayama, a mosquito-net peddler from Tamba, a clothing merchant from Kyoto, and a diviner from the shrine at Kashima. What makes travel on a ferry so interesting is the fact that all the passengers come from different places.

Then the mate shouted: "All aboard! We're shoving off!" The sailors all said their prayers for a safe voyage and, requesting donations for the god of the sea at Sumiyoshi, they passed a collection cup around. There was a count of heads, and everyone present, whether he drank or not, was forced to contribute seven pennies. The sailors dipped saké from a bucket with soup bowls, not bothering to heat it. To go with the saké they had dried flying fish, which they tore apart with their fingers. They gulped their wine down quickly and it soon put them in good spirits.

"Good luck to everyone!" the mate shouted. "Now let's hoist our sails, for the wind is due astern." And they leaned their sails thirty degrees into the wind.

Soon the ship was well over two miles from shore

Then suddenly a courier from Bizen snapped his fingers in anger and cried: "Damn it! I forgot something! I tied my mailbag to my sword and then left it at the inn." He stared at the shore and wailed that he had left his sword leaning against the side of a little Buddhist shrine at the inn.

The others aboard ship shouted at him: "No matter how loud you wail, they can't hear you from here. What kind of man are you, wailing that way? Are you a sissy without any goldballs?"

The courier carefully examined himself and then declared: "I certainly do have—two!"

Everyone burst out laughing, and then one of the sailors said: "I guess there's nothing to do but to turn the ship back." So they reversed rudder and went back into the harbor.

The passengers were angry at this turn of events and cried: "It looks as if we're off to a bad start today."

When the ship reached the shore, men sent from Himeji in pursuit of Seijuro and Onatsu were raising a great commotion, searching everywhere. "Maybe they're aboard this ship," they cried.

Onatsu and Seijuro, unable to hide themselves, lamented: "What a terrible thing has befallen us!"

But their pursuers, insensible to pity, did not even

The others aboard ship shouted at him: "No matter how loud you wail, they can't hear you from here. What kind of man are you, wailing that way? Are you a sissy without any goldballs?"...

listen. Onatsu was placed in a closely guarded litter while Seijuro was bound and taken back to Himeji. Everyone who saw the two weeping and wailing could not help feeling sorry for them.

From that day on Seijuro was shut up in a room, with guards watching over him. Even in the midst of his own miseries, however, he never gave a thought to himself, murmuring only the name of Onatsu, over and over.

"If that rascal had not forgotten his mailbag, Onatsu and I would be together now in Osaka. We would have rented a secluded room in the Kozu section, with only some half-blind old woman for our servant. Onatsu and I agreed that for the first fifty days we would sleep by each other's side day and night, never parting. But that is, alas, all a thing of the past now. I wish they would kill me. Every day is so long—I am weary, weary of life."

And as these thoughts went through his mind, a thousand times or more, he would bite his tongue and shut his eyes tight, in the resolution to die, but then yearning for Onatsu would come back to him and he would think: "Perhaps I will be able to see her again, in all her beauty, in one last parting." He paid no heed to the shame of living on or to what slander people would utter about him. This is what it means

for a man to weep. Even his guards were sad to see
him thus, and tried in every way to remonstrate with
him as the days passed.

Onatsu was in the same sad state. For seven days
she refused food. Then one day she wrote a request
to the god of Murotsu, asking that Seijuro's life be
spared.

Strange to say, that night about midnight an old
man appeared at her bedside, a wondrous oracle who
proclaimed: "Listen well to what I say to you. When
people are sad they usually make such unreasonable
requests that, deity though I am, I am unable to fulfill
them. Some pray to be made rich overnight. Some
covet other people's wives. Some want to kill the
people they hate. Some want the rain changed to
sunny weather. Some even want the nose they were
born with to be a little bigger. Everyone wants something else. They all pray in vain to Buddha and to
the gods, even though their requests cannot possibly
be granted, thus making nuisances of themselves.

"During the last festival there were eighteen thousand and sixteen people who came to worship me.
There wasn't one of that number who didn't pray
greedily for some personal profit. I find their requests
very amusing, but since they throw money at my feet
I am glad to listen, as a god should. Among the

worshipers who visited me, there was only one sincere person. She was a servant from a charcoal shop in Takasago. She bowed to me and said: 'I have no special wish, but hope only that I will continue to be in good health. I will come back to worship you again.' So saying, she left, only to return the next moment and add: 'I would also like you to get me a good-looking man.' I answered her: 'Make requests of that nature to the god at the Shrine of Izumo; I don't know anything about that sort of thing.' But she didn't hear me and went away.

"If you, too, had taken a husband in accordance with the wishes of your parents, you would not have had anything to worry you, but because you are so particular in love, you have fallen into this trouble. Your life, for which you care so little, will be a long one. Seijuro, whose life means so much to you, will soon come to the end of his days."

The dream was so real that it made Onatsu wretched. When she opened her eyes she felt so miserable that she wept until dawn.

Then, just as was expected, Seijuro was summoned and examined, but on unforeseen charges. Seven hundred *ryo* in gold pieces which had been left in a cabinet in a storeroom of the Tajima-ya had disappeared. The story was spread that Seijuro had had

Onatsu steal the money and had then made off with it. Circumstantial evidence was against Seijuro and he was unable to explain the matter. Therefore, sad to say, he was put to death on the eighteenth of April, at the age of twenty-five.

"That is the way of the Fleeting World," thought the people who saw the execution, and their tears wet their sleeves more than an evening shower could have. There was no one of them who did not feel sad and lament the fate of Seijuro.

Later, at the beginning of June, when there was a general cleaning and airing, the place where the seven hundred gold pieces had been put was disturbed, and the money tumbled out of a big chest.

"It just goes to show you how careful you must be," said an old graybeard in the family with an air of "I told you so!"

5. *The seven hundred gold pieces that were found too late*

To know nothing is to know the peace of Buddha, and Onatsu had not yet learned of Seijuro's passing. But one day, as she was thinking of him, some village children came down the street hand-in-hand, singing: "When you kill Seijuro, kill Onatsu too." Hearing this, Onatsu was troubled. She went to ask her childhood nurse what it meant, but the nurse was unable to answer and burst into tears.

"It's true, then!" Onatsu cried out in a frenzy. "Better to die than to live on like this, thinking of him." Whereupon the crazed Onatsu joined in with the children to lead the singing. People pitied her, saying this and that to make her stop, but there was no hope of restraining her now. Their entreaties brought only a deluge of tears from Onatsu.

> *"The man who passes yonder—*
> *Is he not Seijuro?*
> *The reed hat he wears—*
> *Just like Seijuro!*
> *Yahan, ha, ha—"*

Her song ended in a wild, weird laugh. She had lost her senses; her graceful young form was ravaged by madness. She wandered out into the hills and, when it grew dark, lay down in the fields to sleep. One by one the women who went with her there were themselves infected by the same delirious fever, and later all went mad.

Meanwhile, those who had known Seijuro through

the years began to think of giving his remains a proper burial. His body, stained like the blood-soaked grass on which it fell, was washed clean and buried. Above it, as a marker, they planted an oak tree and a pine, and people called the spot "Seijuro's Mound." Nothing could be more pathetic, even in this pitiful world.

Each night Onatsu came to mourn and had clear visions of her lover as he had appeared in times past. Thus the days followed, one after another, until upon the hundredth day since his death she sat herself among the dewy grasses of his grave and drew a knife with which to kill herself.

But her women companions seized the knife and said: "Your death would avail nothing now. If your grief is indeed sincere, cut off your hair and join a holy order. To pray for those who will die in the years to come—that is the enlightened way of Buddha, and we shall follow you in it."

Their words soothed Onatsu's heart. "Let us do just as you say," she answered, and each of the women proved her sincerity by steadfast adherence to Onatsu's decision.

They went to the Temple of True Enlightenment, and when admittance had been granted by the superior, Onatsu, just fifteen, changed her summer clothes for garments of black. She became a most worthy nun.

From the valley stream she brought water to the altar each morning, and in the evening, flowers from the mountaintop. Summer nights, by lanternlight, she zealously recited the Great Sutra. People marveled at her piety and spoke of her as the incarnation of Lady Chujo, of whom we hear in legends.[5]

Even Onatsu's brother felt the first stirring of his soul toward enlightenment when he visited her rude retreat. The seven hundred pieces of gold, which had brought so much grief, were contributed for the holding of services for the dead, and he himself went into mourning for Seijuro.

About this time the story of Onatsu was made into a play in the Kyoto-Osaka region, and from there it spread to even the most remote provinces, winding through each town and hamlet as an endless stream of love, on which men might embark with all their cares and float as light as bubbles through the Fleeting World.

[5] *Chujo-hime* (753–781)—daughter of Fujiwara Toyonari; as a nun she is said to have embroidered the famous Taema Mandala, a tapestry showing the various aspects of Amida's Western Paradise.

Book Two

The Barrelmaker
Brimful of
Love

1. The cleaning of a well by a man unhappy in love

Life is short; love is long.

There once was a cooper who, from the coffins he built with his own hands, realized how impermanent the world is. Although he worked his saw and gimlet assiduously for a living, he made very little money and could rent only a thatched hut in Osaka. He lived in a manner befitting the poorer section of Temma.

There was also a girl who surpassed all the others who lived in her remote village. Her complexion was white even to the ears and her feet were not stained by contact with the soil. On New Year's Eve of her thirteenth year her parents were short the sum of silver required as a village tax, which amounted to one-third of their income, and so the girl was sent to serve as a lady's maid in an imposing city-house near Temma.

As time went on her natural disposition and ready

wit came to be appreciated. She was solicitous toward the old couple, pleased the lady of the house, and was well thought of by all the others. Later she was allowed free access to the inner storeroom where all the fine things were kept. Everyone thought so highly of her that it was said: "What would happen to this house if Osen were not around?" This was all because of her intelligence.

Osen knew nothing of the ways of love. She had spent all of her nights in a manner which some might think unworthy of her—alone. Once when a light-hearted fellow pulled her dress she responded with a full-throated shriek, leaving the man to bewail this unfortunate turn of events. After that no man would ever speak flirtingly to her. People may criticize Osen for such behavior, but it would probably be a good thing if all men's daughters acted as she did.

Our story begins on the seventh day of autumn, the Tanabata Festival day, when silk clothes—guaranteed never to have been worn before—are piled up seven high, right sleeve over left, to be rented to celebrants. It is amusing to see how the upper-class ladies celebrate by tying familiar poems to juniper twigs while the poor people decorate their houses with gourds and persimmons on the branch.

This particular day was a special occasion for the

people of the neighborhood because the common well was being cleaned. The people living in rented houses on the side lanes participated in this cleaning and kept water on the boil for tea to be served to the workmen. After most of the dirty water had been scooped out, the bottom of the well was scraped and up came a variety of things mixed in with pebbles. A kitchen knife, the disappearance of which had puzzled people, came to light, and so did a bunch of seaweed into which a needle had been thrust. I wonder why that was done.[1] Then, on further search, more things came up including some old pony-design coppers, a naked doll without a face, a one-sided sword-handle peg of crude workmanship, and a patched-over baby's bib. You can never tell just what you will find at the bottom of an uncovered, outside well.

Then, when the well cleaners got down to the barrel planking close to the spring, an old two-headed nail came loose and the planking came apart. They sent for the cooper we have mentioned to make a new hoop for the barrel. When he had succeeded in stopping up the slowly flowing water, the cooper noticed an old woman with a crooked back who was fondling a live lizard.

[1] To put a curse or cast a spell upon someone an effigy of seaweed with a needle through it was stuck to a tree or cast into a well.

He asked her what it was, and she answered: "This is a newt which just now was brought up from the well. Don't you recognize one when you see it? If you put this lizard in a bamboo tube and burn it, and then sprinkle its ashes in the hair of the person you love, that person will love you in turn." She spoke with a great deal of conviction.

This woman was formerly an abortionist known as Kosan from Myoto Pond, but when this profession was prohibited she gave up her cruel practice and worked at making noodle-flour with a mortar. Because of the hand-to-mouth nature of such an occupation, she had to work so hard that she did not even hear the temple bell sounding the end of the day. However, as she sank lower and lower in the social scale she learned the lesson of karma and she thought more about the future life.

When she told the cooper about the terrible things that would happen to people who did wrong in this world, he paid no attention to her. Rather, he questioned her the more intently about the efficacy of burning a newt to help in one's love affairs.

Naturally, she became more sympathetic as he talked to her with such earnestness, and she finally asked: "Who is it that you love? I won't tell another soul."

The cooper forgot himself, so much was he thinking

of the one he loved, and as he beat on the bottom of the cask he let himself be carried away by his own words, pouring out all of his story to the old woman. "The one I love does not live far away. I love Osen, the maid of the house here. I have sent her a hundred letters without getting a word in reply."

The old woman nodded and said: "You don't need any newts to win her. I can bridge the stream of love for you. I will disperse the clouds and make your love successful in no time at all."

The cooper was surprised to hear her undertake the matter so lightly. "If this will involve a great deal of money, I am afraid I won't be able to supply it, no matter how much I would like to, for this has been a bad season for me. Naturally, if I had the money I wouldn't begrudge it. All I can promise you is a cotton kimono dyed to your liking at New Year's and a set of Nara-hemp clothes of second quality for the midsummer festival of O-Bon. Is it a bargain?"

"Love that can talk that way must be based on selfishness. I am not looking for that sort of thing at all. You know there is a great art in getting a person to feel love for you. In my lifetime I've helped thousands of people, and always with success. I'll see to it that you meet her before the Chrysanthemum Festival in September.

"...If you put this lizard in a bamboo tube and burn it, and
then sprinkle its ashes in the hair of the person you
love, that person will love you in turn." She
spoke with a great deal of conviction....

This set the flames of love burning more fiercely in the cooper's heart and he cried: "My lady, I will supply you with all the firewood you will need to make tea the rest of your life."

In this world no one knows how long a person may live, and it is amusing to think that love should have made him promise so much.

2. *After the dance: a witch in the night*

There are seven mysterious things in the Temma section of Osaka: the umbrella-shaped flame before the Daikyo Temple; the boy without hands at Shimmei Shrine;[2] the topsy-turvy lady at Sonezaki;[3] the phantom noose of Eleventh Avenue; the crying monk of Kawasaki; the laughing cat of Ikeda-machi; and the smouldering Chinese mortar at the Bush-Warbler's Mound. But these are just the magical tricks of old foxes and badgers. Much more to be feared are those demons in human form who play havoc with the lives of ignorant men.

[2] A Shinto shrine frequented by homosexual prostitutes.
[3] Quarter known for its female prostitutes.

Our souls are dark indeed. And it was so dark the twenty-eighth night of July that hanging lanterns threw no light under the eaves of houseroofs. Street dancers, hoping to sustain their revels till dawn, shouted, "Just one more day to dance till the month is over," but they too reluctantly broke up and returned to their homes. Even the vigilant dog of Four Corners fell fast asleep.

At this late hour old Nanny, the mischievous crone in whom the cooper had put his trust, noticed that the entrance to the great landlord's house was still open. She burst in, slammed the door, and tumbled down onto the kitchen floor, crying: "Oh, oh, it's terrible. Give me a drink of water!"

To those within the house she appeared on the brink of death, but her continued breathing encouraged them to call her back to consciousness, and without more ado she came to life.

"What can you have seen that was so terrifying?" asked the landlord's wife and her aged mother-in-law.

"Well, it's a shameful thing for an old woman to admit, but I went out walking the streets tonight. I went to bed early and couldn't get to sleep, so I decided to go see the dancing. My, it was wonderful! I couldn't get enough of it, especially the Kudoki[4] songs

[4] A long ballad in which one tune was repeated over and over.

with rhymes made up using *yama* and *matsu*. There was one fellow down in front of the Nabeshima mansion who sang exactly like Nihei, the great Donen[5] singer of Kyoto.

"I pushed my way through a crowd of men and watched the show with my fan as an eye-shade so that people couldn't see what an old woman I was. But the men knew what was what, even in the dark. I wiggled my old hips in a most flirtatious way and was really quite sexy in this white gown and black sash. But no one so much as pinched my bottom. 'A woman is a sometime thing.'[6]

"So I started home again, my mind recollecting the old days of my youth, and suddenly near your gate I was hailed by a handsome young fellow of twenty-four or twenty-five. He was desperately in love, so tortured by his fatal passion that he had only a day or two to live in this Fleeting World. It was the cruel Osen, he said, upon whom his heart had fixed itself so hopelessly.[7] He swore that within a week after his death his ghost would come to kill every member of this

---

[5] *Donen-bushi*—a type of ballad made popular by Donen Ganzaburo of Kyoto during the Jokyo era (1684–88).

[6] Literally, "a woman is something only as long she is young."

[7] The language used is that associated with a Buddhist belief concerning human passions, according to which obsessions of the soul (*shushin*) will, if unsatisfied or unrelieved during a person's lifetime, return after death to wreak vengeance upon the object of that passion.

household. Oh, he was so frightsome! He had a great nose, his face was flushed with fever, and his eyes gleamed, just as if he were possessed by the *tengu*[8] whose figure is paraded before the Sumiyoshi festival procession. I was so frightened that I had to run in here."

Everyone who had crowded around to hear her story was aghast, and the householder's aged father wept a little.

"To be unhappy in love," he said, "is not unheard of. Osen is old enough to get married now, and we should keep this man in mind if he has a suitable livelihood. Providing he is not a gambler or widow chaser, and is thrifty and frugal, he might make a good choice. Of course, I do not know the man at all, but I can sympathize with him."

By the long silence which followed, it was plain that the others sympathized with him too. The shrewd old hen certainly knew her business when it came to promoting a love affair.

It was now past midnight and, after she had been helped to her feet, old Nanny returned to her hovel. While she lay there plotting her next move, dawn broke through the east window. Nearby she could hear the sound of flint on steel, as a neighbor started up his

[8] Fabulous being represented with wings and an extremely long nose.

fire. Somewhere an infant began to cry. Sleepily the
tenants of that squalid quarter chased out the mos-
quitoes which had slipped through the breaks in their
paper nets and plagued them throughout the night.
One minute the women's fingers were pinching at the
fleas in their underclothes, the next pinching for some
odd coins on the sanctuary shelf with which to buy a
few green vegetables. Still, amidst the bitter struggle
for existence, pleasure could yet be found by those who,
through wedlock, had won partners for their beds. In
what delights may they not have indulged, with
pillows to the south[9] and mattresses in utter disarray,
violating the vigil of Kinoe-ne?[10]

At last the sun rose to shine upon a brisk, breezy
autumn day. The old woman tied her head up in a
towel and treated herself for a headache, calling upon
the services of Dr. Okajima without worrying how
the bill would be paid. She had just served herself
some broth of fresh herbs, when Osen came in from
the back alley to visit her.

"How are you today?" Osen inquired sweetly, as
from her left sleeve she brought forth half a melon

[9] While both husband and wife were alive they slept with their pillows at the southern end of the bed. Widows and widowers placed
their pillows to the north as a sign of mourning.

[10] On this night a vigil was kept in honor of the God of Plenty and
continence was to be observed until midnight. Children conceived at
this tim ɔwere thought to become criminals.

pickled in the Nara style and wrapped in a lotus leaf, which she set down on a bundle of firewood. "Perhaps you would like it with some soy sauce," she said modestly and made to go get it without waiting for the other's thanks.

"Wait," the old woman insisted. "It is because of you that I am about to die before my time, and since I have no daughter of my own, you must pray for me when I am gone." Then, reaching into a hemp basket, she brought out a pair of purple socks with red ribbons and a patched-up rosary bag, from which she removed her divorce papers. The socks and bag she gave to Osen, saying they would be keepsakes.

Impressionable, as most women are, Osen believed the story and wept. "If there is truly someone in love with me, why didn't he come for help from a love-wise person like yourself? If I had known his intentions, I should not have spurned him lightly."

Old Nanny saw that this was as good a time as any to come out with the whole story. "There is no reason to hide anything from you now. He did come to me many times, and the deep sincerity of his love for you was more touching and pitiful than I can say. If you should reject him now, my resentment will fall upon no one but you." She spoke with all the cleverness that years of wide experience had given her, and, as was only to have been expected, Osen soon yielded.

"I shall be glad to meet him anytime," she cried, dizzy with emotion.

Thereupon the old crone, delighted to have obtained such a promise, whispered: "It just occurred to me how you might best meet him. On the eleventh day of August you must make a secret pilgrimage to Ise.[11] Traveling alone together, you would become fast friends and could spend your bedtime hours sweetly, heart murmuring to heart of undying love. And you know," she added casually, "he is not at all bad looking."

Without further persuasion and before she had even seen him, Osen was consumed with love for this man. "Can he write letters himself? Does his hair fall long and pretty behind his head? I suppose, since he is a craftsman, his back may be a little stooped. Well, when we set out from here, I should like to stop at noon in Moriguchi or Hirakata, so we can get a room and go to bed early."

She was babbling on like this when the chief maid-servant was heard calling outside: "Miss Osen, you're wanted!"

[11] It was a popular custom to make the pilgrimage to Ise without the knowledge of one's parents or master. When the pilgrim returned he was supposed to be forgiven, not censured for his act.

"... you must make a secret pilgrimage to Ise. Traveling alone
together, you would become fast friends and could spend
your bedtime hours sweetly, heart murmuring
to heart of undying love...."

Osen quickly took her leave: "It's all set for the eleventh then. . . ."

3. *As delicious as the water of Kyoto: the intimacy of lovers meeting in secret*

"The morning-glories are in bloom and it would be nice to have a look at them tomorrow early—nice and cool, too," the lady of the house added as she began her instructions to the servants that evening. "I want you to arrange some seats out near the back hedge, away from the house. Spread out the flower-mats, put baked rice and toothpicks in the different compartments of the picnic box, and don't forget the tea bottle. I shall take a bath just before six in the morning and then I want my hair done up simply in three plain rolls. As for a gown, let me have the hempen one with open sleeeves and a pink lining. I shall wear my gray-satin sash with circle designs on it, the informal, two-piece one dotted with our family crest. I want you to take the utmost care in everything because we may be seen by people in the adjacent streets. So each of you must dress in decent-looking clothes. A

litter should be sent at the usual rising time to my
sister's house in Tenjinbashi."

She put all the arrangements in the charge of Osen,
who attended the lady upon her retirement into an
ample mosquito net, at the four corners of which little
bells jingled while Osen gently fanned her to sleep.
Imagine so much fuss over nothing but some flowers
in your back yard!

But perhaps such vanity is not the weakness of
women alone. At this time the master of the house
was probably wasting himself and his money on Miss
Nokaze of Shimabara and Miss Ogino of Shimmachi,[12]
buying both of them the same day, one for each end
of his carrying-pole. Though he spoke of visiting Tsu-
mura Temple each morning, and carried a shoulder
pad[13] for that purpose, it is much more likely that
he went straight to the licensed quarter for a morning
of sport and pleasure.

Just before dawn on the eleventh of August old
Nanny heard a light tapping on the door of her shanty.

"It is Osen," the girl outside whispered as she threw
in a bundle which had been hastily wrapped in a large
kerchief. Returning immediately to her master's
house, Osen did not realize that the old crone would

[12] Names used by high-class prostitutes in the licensed quarters of
Kyoto and Osaka respectively.

[13] An item of priestly vestments sometimes carried by lay devotees.

lose no time in searching through the bundle to see what was there: five strings of cash worth about one farthing of silver each, and perhaps eighteen *momme* of pony-engraved silver pieces; nearly a peck of polished rice; a dried bonito; two combs in a charm bag; a one-piece sash of many colors; a silver and brown garment for cooler weather; a lighter gown, well worn, with a fan pattern; cotton socks, the soles of which were unfinished; sandals with loose straps; and a parasol on which Osen had naïvely written her address! The old woman quickly set about erasing the telltale characters in such a way as to leave no unsightly smear upon the parasol. As she did so, someone greeted her from the entranceway.

"Old Nanny, I shall go on ahead now," the cooper called in on his way past.

Later Osen appeared, trembling a little. "Sorry to be late. I was detained at the house."

The old woman then took up the bundle of personal belongings and hastened with Osen down an unfamiliar byway. "It would be a great effort for me, but perhaps for the sake of the pilgrimage I should accompany you to Ise," old Nanny suggested.

Osen was plainly upset. "It's a long trip for an elderly woman and you would find it hard going. Why don't you take the night boat down from Fushimi after you have taken me to meet this man?" she replied tactlessly, for she had now no patience with anything that might upset the headlong progress of her affair.

Just as they were crossing the Capital Bridge, along came Kyushichi, a manservant in the same household as Osen. He had come this way to watch the morning change of guard at Osaka Castle, but, his curiosity aroused when the two women came by, Kyushichi inevitably became a further obstacle in the path of the lovers.

"Why, I have been thinking for some time of making the same pilgrimage and there could be no better companions for the journey than yourselves. Just leave your baggage for me to carry. Fortunately, I have plenty of spending money and can see to it that you suffer no inconvenience on that score." From his excessive politeness one could guess that Kyushichi was inspired by some secret design on Osen, and old Nanny's hostility was immediately aroused.

"A young lady traveling in the company of a man! Now wouldn't that seem most extraordinary to the people who saw us! Besides, the gods of Ise frown on that sort of thing. I have heard and seen enough of people who willfully disgrace themselves before society. Please don't follow us."

"Well, I hardly expected to run into objections of this sort. Believe me, I have no designs on Miss Osen; faith alone moves me to this. In love, the gods will assure my success, without my having to solicit their protection, for my heart is true, true as the road we shall travel together. If the sun and moon favor us and Miss Osen so inclines, we can travel anywhere— to the capital perhaps. This would be just the time to spend four or five days there, seeing the maples of Takao in their bright fall colors and the blooming mushrooms of Saga. The master generally stops at a hotel in Kawara-machi, but I think we would find it awkward there. We could do better," Kyushichi continued as if he would have everything his own way, "by taking some cozy rooms at the western end of Third Avenue. Then the old lady here could visit the Temple of the Original Vow, on Sixth Avenue.

By this time the autumn sun was up over the mountainside, and the travelers were halfway past the pine-shaded banks of the Yodo River when they ran upon a man who looked very conspicuous, seated beneath a cat's-paw willow as if waiting for someone. On closer examination the old crone recognized him as the cooper. From the look in her eyes he could tell that something had gone wrong; it had not worked out as planned after he went on ahead of them.

"You look as if you were going to Ise too," old Nanny addressed him. "But why go alone? You seem to be an agreeable fellow and we'd like to have you spend the night with us somewhere."

The cooper was delighted, of course. "It's so true: 'The kindness of others always brightens a journey.' I am certainly grateful for the invitation."

Kyushichi, on the other hand, looked bewildered. "It seems a little odd, especially with this young lady along, to have someone join us when you don't even know where he's going."

"Oh," the old woman replied, "God watches over everything. And with a stout fellow like you along, what can possibly happen?"

Thereafter the four of them slept in the same inn each night. Kyushichi, watching carefully for any opportunity to satisfy his secret desires, removed one of the sliding doors which separated him from the ladies and would peek in at them on his way to the bath. At night, when the four of them slept in a row, he stretched out his hand and tipped up the oil lamp so as to smother the light.

Then, just as it was about to fail, the cooper exclaimed, "It's awfully warm for fall," and opened the window near him so that bright moonlight shone through upon the four sleeping figures.

Again, when Osen made a pretense of snoring and Kyushichi moved his right leg over upon her, he was quickly detected by the cooper, who promptly started up a song about the Soga brothers, "Love plays mischief with all . . ." while beating time with the end of his fan. Osen then abandoned the pretense of sleeping and started to talk with old Nanny.

"There is nothing so calamitous as to bring a girl-child into the world. I have been thinking that it would be a good idea to become a novice at the Fudo Chapel of Kitano next New Year's and eventually become a nun."

"Very good idea," the crone answerd sleepily. "Better than to live on in a world full of disappointments."

Thus the two men stood in each other's way the whole night through. The upshot of their bedtime activities was only this: that Kyushichi, who started the evening with his pillow to the west, wriggled around and wound up with his head to the south and his underclothing missing—a shocking piece of carelessness for a pilgrim with money in his waistband; while the cooper slept with a resentful scowl on his face, a wad of tissue paper in his hand, and a clamshell full of clove oil[14] beside him.

The next morning at Mt. Osaka they hired an Otsu

[14] Used like toilet water.

man's horse and proceeded on their journey with Osen
riding in the middle and the men mounted on either
side of her. Funny though an onlooker would have
found this arrangement, there was something, whether
fatigue or simply pleasure, which made the riders
oblivious to their absurdity. On one side Kyushichi
fondled Osen's toes; on the other the cooper reached
up and put his arm around her waist; and each playfully indulged his secret desires as best he could in a
manner that seems somewhat amusing to anyone who
knows what each was after.

None of the group had any real interest in the pilgrimage itself. At Ise they failed to visit the Inner
Shrine or the sacred beach at which homage is paid to
the Sun, stopping only at the Outer Shrine for a few
minutes and purchasing as their only souvenirs a puri-
fication broach and some seaweed.

On the way back the two men kept their eyes on
each other, so nothing of consequence happened. When
they reached the capital, Kyoto, and Kyushichi had
guided them to the hotel he knew, the cooper reckoned
in his head what he owed Kyushichi for bills the latter
had paid, thanked him for his trouble, and took his
leave with a bow. Thinking that he would henceforth
have Osen to himself, Kyushichi went out and bought
many presents and souvenirs for her. He could hardly

On one side Kyushichi fondled Osen's toes; on the other the cooper reached up and put his arm around her waist; and each playfully indulged his secret desires as best he could in a manner that seems somewhat amusing....

*None of the group had any real interest in the pilgrimage
itself. At Ise they failed to visit the Inner Shrine
or the sacred beach ... stopping only at the
Outer Shrine for a few minutes....*

wait for night to fall, but decided to while away the time visiting someone he knew in the neighborhood of Karasumaru.

In the meantime old Nanny left the hotel with Osen, ostensibly to visit Kiyomizu Temple. They went directly to Gion-machi, to a little shop which sold box lunches, and there found a card upon which was written "Gimlet and Saw." Recognizing this as the cooper's way of identifying himself, Osen slipped inside almost unnoticeably. Upstairs she found her lover, and together they drank the cup of betrothal, pledging themselves to each other forever.

Thereupon old Nanny retired downstairs. "The water here is simply delicious," she exclaimed as she guzzled cups of tea one after another.

Having won from Osen the first installment on their marriage, the cooper left early for Osaka by day boat. Old Nanny and Osen, upon their return to the hotel, gave notice of immediate departure. Kyushichi pleaded with them to stay for a few more days of sightseeing, but the old woman was determined.

"No, no. What would your mistress say if she thought Osen was chasing around with men?" So off they started.

"I know it's a lot to ask, but this bundle is so heavy. Won't you help us with it, Kyushichi?"

"My back aches. Sorry," he replied.

And when they stopped to rest in a wisteria grove before the Great Buddha of Inari, the women had to pay for their own tea.

4. *Shingles kindle a fire in the heart, and so in the hearth*

"If you had told us you wanted to go on a pilgrimage, we would have sent you in a litter or on hired horse-back. But to make a secret pilgrimage in the fantastic way you did, and come back with all these presents bought by lord knows whom—why, it's—it's just the sort of thing one never does, not even married couples. And traveling to the capital together, drinking and sleeping together—who would dare go that far?

"Osen is just a woman, and it may be too much to expect that she could resist the urgings of Kyushichi. But Kyushichi, the smart aleck, thinks he must teach the innocent gods what manliness is, and teach this innocent girl . . ."

Their mistress was in a frightful rage. Kyushichi's explanations had no effect on her at all, and the poor, guiltless fellow was finally discharged, without waiting for the regular biannual replacement time of September fifth. Later he worked several terms in a wholesale house called Bizen-ya in Kitano and married a drifter[15] named Longie of Eighthbridge. Now he earns a living as a *sushi*[16] vendor on Willow Lane and has simply forgotten about Osen.

Osen went back to the uneventful routine of household duties, but she was unable to forget her brief romance with the cooper or get him out of her mind. She began to neglect herself, becoming shabby in appearance, careless in conduct, and little by little more gaunt and pale. Finally, losing control of herself, Osen started to wail throughout the night like a sick hen.

About the same time a series of further misfortunes overtook the household. The great cauldron rusted so that its bottom fell out; there was a sudden change between breakfast and supper in the taste of the prepared bean-paste; and lightning struck the roof of the storehouse, setting fire to the shingles. All of these things had a perfectly natural explanation, but people felt that in this case they had some special significance. Someone said: "It is the implacable spirit of the man who is madly in love with Osen—the cooper."

---

[15] Literally, "lotus-leaf woman"—a prostitute hired by a business organization to entertain traveling merchants. She floated, like a lotus leaf on the water, from one man to another.

[16] Cakes of cold, cooked rice topped with eggs, fish, etc.

When her master and mistress heard this, they decided to do everything in their power to bring Osen and the cooper together in wedlock. Nanny was called in for a consultation.

"Osen," the old crone said craftily, "has told me several times that she would not have a hand laborer for a husband, and she isn't sure whether or not the cooper will do. But it seems to me that she is being unnecessarily choosy. If, in spite of all, they can just get along in life together, she should be satisfied."

Having heard old Nanny's ideas on the subject, Osen's employers sent for the cooper and concluded a marriage contract with him. Soon afterward, Osen had her sleeves sewn up and her teeth blackened in preparation for the marriage, an auspicious date for which had already been chosen. Her dowry consisted of twenty-three items, including a second-grade chest with a natural finish, a wicker hamper for her trousseau, a folding pasteboard box, two castoff gowns from her mistress, quilted bedclothes, a mosquito net with red lining, and a scarf of classic colors. With all of these, more than a pound of silver was sent to the cooper's house.

The newlyweds proved quite compatible and their luck was good. Honest and industrious, the husband kept his head bent assiduously over the work of his

Soon afterward, Osen had her sleeves sewn up and her teeth blackened in preparation for the marriage, an auspicious date for which had already been chosen. Her dowry consisted of twenty-three items....

craft, while his good wife took up weaving striped cloth
of dark-dyed Fushikane thread. Night and day they
worked and never failed to meet their debts on the
last day of the year or the day before the Bon Festival.
Osen took especially good care of the cooper. In winter,
on windy days or when it snowed, she carefully covered
his rice to keep it warm when he took it out. In
summer she kept a fan close to her pillow to cool him
with. When he was out of the house she locked the
gate and never looked at another man. If she had occasion to speak of anything, it was always "my husband
this, my husband that." Even when, after several years
and months, she bore two children, Osen did not forsake her husband for them.

Alas, however, most women are fickle creatures.
Captivated by some delicious love story, or deluded by
the latest dramatic productions of Dotom-bori[17] their
souls are caught up in giddy corruption. Amidst the
falling cherry blossoms of the Temple of the Heavenly
Kings or under a blooming wisteria trellis, they fall
head over heels in love with some handsome fellow.
And so, upon returning home, they find loathsome the
man who has supported them for many long years.

There is no greater folly than this. From the
moment of their seduction such women abandon all

[17] Theatre section of Osaka.

prudence and frugality, light great fires in their ovens and leave them untended, burn lamps thoughtlessly where no lamp is needed, and while their family fortunes dwindle, wait impatiently for leisure hours to spend away from home. Such marriages are dreadful indeed.

And should their husbands die, in seven days these women are out looking for other husbands. Divorced once, they marry and divorce again, six or seven times. That, unfortunately, is what the morals of the lower classes have sunk to, but this sort of thing, of course, never ever happens among the upper classes. A woman should give herself to only one man during her lifetime. If trouble arises or misfortune strikes, even when she is young, it is quite possible for her to become a nun in the Convent of Kaga or in the Hokkeji Nunnery of the Southern Capital, for this has been done many times before.

There are many others in the Fleeting World who live in sin with secret lovers, but when they are discovered, either their husbands send them home without taking the matter to court, for fear of creating a sensation, or, in the case of husbands greedy for gold, some kind of deal is made and the matter dropped. Thus sinful women are spared through laxity in punishment, and for this reason adultery cannot be stamped out.

But there are gods and there is retribution. Every secret will be made known. How much to be dreaded —this ruinous road!

5. *Life is shorter than a toothpick made from woodshavings*

This is to announce an informal supper party to be held at my home on the sixteenth next. I should greatly appreciate having the honor of your company. P.S. Guests not listed in order of local prominence.[18]

Chozaemon, the yeast maker, found the years and months passing as if life were only a dream. Already it was fifty years since his father died, and he had reason to congratulate himself on living long enough to celebrate such an anniversary. According to the ancients: "When one goes into mourning on the fiftieth anniversary of his father's death, it is customary to abstain from meat in the morning, but eat fish for supper and drink and sing throughout the evening, having thereafter no further obligations to perform."

[18] The same invitation was sent to all guests. Frequently their names were listed in order of prominence, but this formality could be dispensed with by adding the above note.

Since these were to be the last services, Chozaemon did not begrudge a little expense in conducting them properly. The wives of the neighborhood joined in the preparations. They got out the wooden bowls, trays, crockery, and different kinds of wooden plates used only on special occasions, dusted them, and set them on the sideboard.

It happened that the cooper's wife was on friendly terms with these people, so she too dropped in to offer her services. "Isn't there some work to be done in the kitchen?"

Osen was known as an intelligent and capable person, and they gave her a delicate job. "There are some sweets in the bedroom. Set them out on the deep trays."

Osen began her job of arranging the imperial persimmons, Chinese walnuts, falling-goose candies, and toothpicks of kaya and cryptomeria wood. When she was almost finished, Master Chozaemon came in to fetch a nest of bowls from the shelf, but in doing so he clumsily dropped one on Osen's head so that her hairdo came apart all at once. He apologized profusely.

"Oh, it didn't hurt at all," Osen assured him as she hastily tied up her hair and went into the kitchen.

When the lady of the house saw her, however, she was immediately aroused. "Until a few minutes ago your hair was done up most beautifully. How could it become disarranged so suddenly?"

Osen, with a clear conscience, replied calmly: "The master was taking some bowls down from the shelf and one fell on me. That's how it happened."

But the lady would not believe her at all. "Indeed! A bowl falling off the shelf in broad daylight! What a playful bowl that must be. If you ask me, somebody fell into bed without going to sleep and her hair came undone. Of all things for an older man to be doing, when he is supposed to be mourning for his father!"

In a violent rage, she picked up some slices of fresh fish, which had been cut and arranged with much care, and began throwing them about the kitchen. No matter what anyone else talked of during the day, vinegar or flour or anything, she would drag in the subject of Osen and not let it drop, to the complete disgust of all who heard about the incident later. Truly it is the greatest of misfortunes for a man to have a wife of such fierce jealousy.

At first Osen put up patiently with the lady's ranting, though she could not help being annoyed by it. Later, the more she thought about it the more bitter and depressed Osen became. "My sleeve is already wet with tears. Having suffered the shame, there is nothing left to lose. I shall make love to Chozaemon and teach

"...If you ask me, somebody fell into bed without going to
sleep and her hair came undone. Of all things for an
older man to be doing, when he is supposed
to be mourning for his father!"...

that woman a lesson." And, dwelling upon this idea, she aroused in herself a passion for Chozaemon which soon resulted in a secret exchange of promises between the two. They waited only for a suitable occasion to fulfill their desires.

The evening of January twenty-second, in the second year of Tokyo (1685), seemed a propitious one for lovers since the women and children of the neighborhood were amusing themselves at the traditional spring pastime of drawing strings for prizes. On into the night they played, completely absorbed in the game. Some lost and quit, others won and kept on with insatiable enthusiasm. Still others dozed off and started to snore. The cooper turned down his lamp and went to bed early, apparently so tired from the day's toil that he would not have awakened even if someone had pinched his nose.

Chozaemon followed Osen home from the party. "Now is the time to fulfill our mutual promise," he urged, and Osen, unable to refuse him, took Chozaemon into her house.

Then began what was to be their first and last attempt at love-making.

No sooner had they removed their underclothes than the cooper awoke. "Hold on! If I catch you, I'll never let you go!" he shouted.

Chozaemon quickly threw off the bedcovers. Naked and terrified, he dashed out and ran a great distance to the house of a close relative, barely escaping with his life.

Osen, realizing that it was a hopeless situation for her, plunged the blade of a carpenter's plane into her heart and died. Her corpse was exposed in the Shame Field with that of the scoundrel Chozaemon when he was at last executed. Their names, known in countless ballads and songs, spread to distant provinces with the warning: This is a stern world and sin never goes unpunished.

Book Three

What the Seasons
Brought the Al-
manac Maker

1. The beauty contest

According to the calendar for the second year of Tenwa (1682), New Year's Day was to be devoted to the practice of calligraphy. Then, having started the year auspiciously, men could start making love on January second. Since the Age of the Gods love-making has been taught men by the wagtail bird[1] and ever since those days it has caused endless mischief between the sexes.

In Kyoto lived a lady known as the Almanac-Maker's Beautiful Spouse, who stirred up a mountain of passion in the capital and figured again and again in notorious romances. Her moon-shaped eyebrows rivaled in beauty the crescent borne aloft during the Gion Festival parade; her figure suggested the cherry

[1] Literally, the "love-knowing bird." It taught the ways of love to the gods Izanagi and Izanami, the parents of the Sun Goddess.

buds, not yet blossoms, of Kiyomizu; and her lovely lips looked like the topmost leaves of the maples at Takao in their full autumnal glory. She lived in Muromachi-dori, the style center for women of discriminating taste in clothes, the most fashionable district in all Kyoto.

It was late spring; men felt gay and the wisteria hung like a cloud of purple over Yasui, robbing the pines of their color. People thronged up Higashi-yama and turned it into a living mountain of human figures. There was in the capital a band of four inseparable young men who were known for their handsome appearance and riotous living. Thanks to large inheritances, they could spend every day in the year seeking their own pleasure. One night, till dawn, they might amuse themselves in Shimabara with Chinagirl, Fragrance, Florapoint, and Highbridge. Next day they might make love to Takenaka Kichisaburo, Karamatsu Kasen, Fujita Kichisaburo, and Mitsuse Sakon[2] in the Shijo-gawara section. Night or day, girls or boys, it made no difference in their pleasure.

After the theatre one evening they were lounging around a teahouse called the Matsu-ya and one of them remarked: "I have never seen so many good-looking local girls as I did today. Do you suppose we

²Actors famous for their female impersonations.

could find others who would seem just as beautiful now?

They thought they might and decided to watch for pretty girls among the people who had gone to see the wisteria blossoms and were now returning to their homes. After a worldly actor in the group had been chosen as chief judge, a "beauty contest" was conducted until the twilight hours, providing a new source of amusement for the jaded gentlemen.

At first they were disappointed to see some maids riding in a carriage which hid them from sight. Then a group of girls strolled by in a rollicking mood—"not bad, not bad at all"—but none of the girls quite satisfied their exacting standards. Paper and ink had been brought to record the entries, and it was agreed that only the best should be put on their list.

Next they spied a lady of thirty-three or thirty-four with a long, graceful neck and intelligent-looking eyes, above which could be seen a natural hairline of rare beauty. Her nose, it was true, stood a little high, but that could be easily tolerated. Underneath she wore white satin; over that, light-blue satin; and outside, reddish-yellow satin. Each of these garments was luxuriously lined with the same material. On her left sleeve was a hand-painted likeness of the Yoshida monk, along with this passage: "To sit alone under a

They...decided to watch for pretty girls among the people who had gone to see the wisteria blossoms and were now returning to their homes...providing a new source of amusement for the jaded gentlemen....

lamp, and read old books . . ."[3] Assuredly, this was a woman of exquisite taste.

Her sash was of folded taffeta bearing a tile design. Around her head she had draped a veil like that worn by court ladies; she wore stockings of pale silk and sandals with triple-braided straps. She walked noiselessly and gracefully, moving her hips with a natural rhythm.

"What a prize for some lucky fellow!" one of the young bucks exclaimed. But these words were hardly uttered when the lady, speaking to an attendant, opened her mouth and disclosed that one of her lower teeth was missing, to the complete disillusionment of her admirers.

A little behind her followed a maiden not more than fifteen or sixteen years old. On the girl's left was a woman who appeared to be her mother; on the right she was accompanied by a black-robed nun. There were also several servant women and a footman as escorts, all taking the greatest care of their charge. It seemed at first as if the girl were engaged to be mar-

[3] Yoshida no Kaneyoshi, known as Kenko (1283–1350?). A court official who returned to live as a hermit and write the *Tsurezure-Gusa*, from which this passage is taken. The complete passage: "To sit alone in the lamplight with a good book spread out before you and hold intimate converse with men of unseen generations—such is a pleasure beyond compare." Sansom, *Transactions of the Asiatic Society of Japan*, Vol. 37, p. 17

ried, but at second glance she proved to be married already, for her teeth were blackened and her eyebrows removed. She was quite pretty, with her round face, intelligent eyes, ears delicately draped at the side of her head, and fingers, plump, thin-skinned, and white. She wore clothes with matchless elegance; underneath were purple-spotted fawns on a field of pure yellow; outside, the design of a hundred sparrows upon gray satin. Over her rainbow-colored sash she wore a breast-belt which enhanced the charm of her carriage. The tie-strings of her richly lined rainhat were made from a thousand braids of twisted paper. They could easily see under the hat—a delight for the eyes, or so they thought until someone noticed a wide scar, three inches or more, on the side of her face. She could hardly have been born with such a deformity, and they all laughed when one of the playboys remarked: "She must really hate the nurse who is responsible for that!"

Then another girl, perhaps twenty or twenty-one, came along wearing a garment of cotton homespun, even the lining of which was so tattered and patched that the wind, blowing it out, exposed her poverty to all. The material for her sash came from an old coat and was pitifully thin. She wore socks of purple leather, apparently the only kind she could afford, and tough, rough Nara sandals. An old cloth headpiece was stuck on the top of her head. It was anybody's guess how long ago the teeth of a comb had run through her hair, which fell in sloppy disarray, relieved hardly at all by her haphazard attempts to tuck it up.

But while she made no pretensions to style or fashion, the girl, walking alone, seemed to be enjoying herself. As far as her facial features were concerned, she certainly left nothing to be desired; indeed, the men were captivated by the sight of her.

"Have you ever seen anyone with so much natural beauty?"

"If she had some fine clothes to wear, that girl would steal men's hearts away. Too bad that she should have to be born poor."

They pitied her deeply and one fellow, seeing that she was on her way home, followed hopefully to learn who she was. "She is the wife of a tobacco-cutter down at the end of Seiganji-dori," someone told him. It was disappointing—another straw of hope gone up in smoke!

Later a woman of twenty-six or twenty-seven passed that way. Her arms were covered by three layers of sleeves, all of black silk and lined in red. Her family crest was done in gold, but discreetly, on the inner lining, so as to be faintly visible through the sleeves.

She had on a broad sash which tied in front and was made from dark-striped cloth woven in China. Her hair was rolled up in a bun, set further back on the head than was the case with unmarried ladies, and done up with a thick hair-ribbon and two combs. Covering it was a hand-painted scarf and a rainhat in the style of Kichiya,[4] also set jauntily back on her head so as not to hide the good looks in which she obviously took pride. Her figure twisted sinuously as she stepped lightly along.

"That's the one, that's the one!"

"Quiet down! Let's get a better look at her."

Sure enough, on closer inspection they found that the lady was accompanied by three servants, each carrying a baby.

"Must have had three kids in three years."

Behind her the babies kept calling out "Mama, mama," while the lady walked on, pretending not to hear them.

"They may be her children, but she would just as soon not be seen with them. 'Charm fades with childbirth!' people say." Thus the men shouted and laughed and ridiculed her, until she almost died of chagrin.

[4] An actor famous for his female roles in Kyoto during the Empo era (1673–81) who set many styles in lady's wear.

Next, with a litter borne luxuriously beside her, came a twelve- or thirteen-year-old girl whose hair was combed out smooth, curled a bit at the ends, and tied down with a red ribbon. In front her hair was parted like a young boy's and held in place by five immaculate combs and a gold hair-ribbon. Her face was perfectly beautiful, and I shall not tire you with needless details. A black, ink-slab pattern adorned her white-satin chemise; a peacock design could be perceived in the iridescent satin of her outer garment. Over this hung lace made from Chinese thread and sleeves which were beautifully designed. A folded sash of twelve colors completed her ensemble. Her bare feet nestled in paper-strap clogs, and one of the litter-bearers carried a stylish rainhat for her.

The girl was holding a bunch of wisteria blossoms over her head, as if to attract the attention of someone who could not find her. Observed in this pose, she was clearly the most beautiful girl of all they had seen that day.

"What is the name of this fine lady?" they asked politely of an attendant.

"A girl from Muro-machi," was the reply. "She is called Modern Komachi."[5]

---

[5] The modern equivalent of Ono-no-Komachi, a poetess and famous beauty who was for a time the favorite of the Emperor Nimmyo (834–50) and thereafter spurned all other suitors, finally dying a beggar.

Yes, she had all the beauty of a flower. Only later did they learn how much devilry was hid beneath that beauty.

2. The sleeper who slipped up

The life of a bachelor has its attractions, but nights get rather lonely for a man without a wife. So it seemed to a certain maker of almanacs[6] who had lived alone for many years. There were many elegant ladies in the capital, but his heart was set on finding a woman of exceptional beauty and distinction, and such a desire was not easily satisfied. Finally, in despair because of his solitary existence, he asked some relatives to find him a suitable mate, and it was arranged for him to meet the girl known as Modern Komachi, that delicate beauty holding wisteria blossoms over her head whom our playboys had seen during their beauty contest in the theatre section last spring.

The almanac maker was completely charmed with

[6] *Daikyoji*—originally an expert in the mounting of scrolls and paintings, a fairly high-class profession since it was associated with religious institutions. At this time the *daikyoji* was also the official almanac publisher for the court.

her. "She's the one," he told himself, and without more ado he rushed out, ludicrously enough, to arrange an immediate marriage. At the corner of Shimotachi-uri and Karasumaru he found an old woman, a professional go-between who was widely known as a very fast talker. Thanks to her, the negotiations were conducted successfully. A keg of saké was sent to confirm the contract and on the appointed day Osan was welcomed into her new home.

Deeply attached to his wife and absorbed in the intimacies of their life together, the almanac maker was blind to everything else—to the flower-fragrant nights of spring and to the rising of the autumn moon. Night and day for three years his wife diligently performed the many tasks which married life required of her, carefully spinning raw-silk thread by hand, supervising the weaving of cloth by her servant women, looking after her husband's personal appearance, burning as little fuel as possible for economy's sake, and keeping her expense accounts accurate and up-to-date. In fact, she was just the sort of woman any townsman would want in his home.

Their house was prospering and their companionship seemed to hold a store of endless bliss, when it became necessary for the almanac maker to travel to Edo for business reasons. The parting was sad, but there was nothing to be gained by grieving over it. When he was ready to leave, he paid a visit to Osan's father in Muro-machi to tell him about the trip, and the old man was quite concerned about his daughter's welfare during the period of her husband's absence, when she would be left to manage all of his affairs. He wondered if there were not some capable person who could take over the master's business and also assist Osan in running the household. Deciding on a young man named Moemon, who had served him faithfully for many years, he sent the fellow to his son-in-law's place.

This Moemon was honest and extremely frugal, so much so that he completely neglected his personal appearance, even economizing on his coat sleeves, which measured only two and one-half inches at the wrist. His forehead was narrow, and when upon his reaching manhood his hair was allowed to grow, Moemon never bothered to buy a hat to cover it. Moreover, he went about without the protection of a short sword and slept with his abacus under his head, the better perhaps to reckon how great a fortune he could amass in a night spent dreaming of money-making.

It was fall, and a bitter storm one night set Moemon to thinking how he might fortify himself against the rigors of winter. He decided on a treatment of moxa cauterizing.[7]   A maidservant named Rin, who was adept at administering the burning pills, was asked to do the job for him.   She twisted several wads of the cottony herb and spread a striped bedcover over her dressing table for Moemon to lie on.

The first couple of applications were almost more than he could bear.   The pain-wracked expression on his face gave great amusement to the governess, the house-mistress, and all the lowly maids around him. When further doses had been applied, he could hardly wait for the final salting down which would finish the treatment.   Then, accidentally, some of the burning fibers broke off and dropped down along his spine, causing his flesh to tighten and shrink a little.   But out of consideration for the girl who attended him, Moemon closed his eyes, clenched his teeth, and mustered up all his patience to endure the pain.

Rin, full of sympathy for him, extinguished the vagrant embers and began to massage his skin.   How could she have known that this intimate contact with his body would arouse in her a passionate desire for Moemon, which at first she managed to conceal from others but eventually was to be whispered about and even reach her mistress' ears?

[7] Moxa—in Japanese *mogusa*—a cottony herb placed on the skin and burned as a cauterizing agent. The treatment is still regarded in some parts of China and Japan as beneficial for a wide variety of ailments.

*Rin, full of sympathy for him, extinguished the vagrant embers
and began to massage his skin. How could she have
known that this intimate contact with his body
would arouse in her a passionate desire? ...*

Unable to suppress her desire for Moemon, Rin hoped that somehow she might communicate with him, but as her education had only been of the most humble sort, she could not write anything, not even the crude-looking characters which Kyushichi, a fellow servant, used to scribble out as personal reminders. She asked Kyushichi if he would write a letter for her, but the knave only took advantage of her confidence by trying to make this love his own.

So, slowly, the days passed without relief, and fall came, with its long twilight of drizzling rains, the spawning season for intrigue and deception. One day, having just finished a letter to her husband in Edo, Osan playfully offered to write a love letter for Rin. With her brush she dashed off a few sweet lines of love, and then, addressing the wrapper "To Mr. Mo——, from someone who loves him," Osan gaily turned the note over to Rin.

Overjoyed, the girl kept looking for a suitable opportunity to deliver it, when all at once Moemon was heard calling from the shop for some fire with which to light his tobacco. Fortunately there was no one else in the courtyard at that time, so Rin seized the occasion to deliver her letter in person.

Considering the nature of the thing, Moemon failed to notice his mistress' handwriting and simply took Rin for a very forward girl, certainly an easy conquest. Roguishly he wrote out a reply and handed it to Rin, who was of course unable to read it and had to catch Osan in a good mood before she could learn its contents:

"In response to the unexpected note which your feelings toward me prompted you to write, I confess that, young as I am, your advances are not wholly distasteful to me. I must remind you that such trysts as you propose may produce complications involving a midwife, but if you are ready to meet all of the expenses incidental to the affair—clothes, coats, bath money, and personal toiletries—I shall be glad to oblige to the best of my ability."

"Such impudence!" Osan exclaimed when she finished reading the blunt message to Rin. "There is no dearth of men in this world, and Rin is hardly the worst-looking of all women. She can have a man like Moemon anytime she wants."

Thus aroused, Osan decided to write further importunate messages for Rin and make Moemon her loving slave. So she sent several heartbreaking appeals to him, moving Moemon to pity and then to passion. At last, to make up for his earlier impertinence, he wrote Rin an earnest note in reply. It contained a promise that on the night of May fourteenth, when it was customary to stay up and watch the full moon, he would definitely come to see her.

Mistress Osan laughed aloud when she saw this and told the assembled maids: "We shall turn his big night into a night of fun for all!"

Her plan was to take the place of Rin that night, disguise herself in cotton summer-clothes, and lie in Rin's bed. It was also arranged for the various women-servants to come running with sticks and staves and lanterns when Osan called out.

Thus all were ready and in their places when the time came, but before she knew it, Osan herself fell blissfully asleep, and the women-servants too, exhausted by all the excitement that evening, dozed off and started to snore.

Later, during the early-morning hours, Moemon stole through the darkness with his underclothes hanging half-loose around him. Impatiently he slipped naked between the bedcovers; his heart throbbed, but his lips were silent. And when his pleasure was had, Moemon sensed the faint, appealing fragrance which arose from the lady's garments. He lifted up the covers and started to tiptoe away.

"Indeed, she must know more of life than I suspected. I thought she was innocent, that she had loved no man before, that now—but someone has been here ahead of me," he concluded apprehensively. "I must pursue this no further."

When he had gone Osan awoke of her own accord. To her surprise the pillows were out of place and everything was in disorder. Her sash, missing from her waist, was nowhere at hand, her bed-tissues were a mess.

Overcome with shame at the realization of her undoing, Osan considered: "There is no way to keep this from others. From now on I may as well abandon myself to this affair, risk my life, ruin my reputation, and take Moemon as my companion on a journey to death."

She confided this resolution to Moemon, and though it was contrary to his previous decision, nevertheless, being halfway in and feeling the call to love, Moemon gave himself over to visiting her each night without a care for the reproofs of others, and spent himself in this new service as thoroughly as he had in his work. Thus, together the lovers played with life and death, the most dangerous game of all.

3. *The lake which took people in*

It is written in *The Tale of Genji:* "There is no logic to love."

When the image of Kannon was put on display at the Ishiyama Temple the people of Kyoto left the cherry blossoms of Higashi-yama and flocked to see it. Travelers, on their way to and from the capital, stopped for a visit when they crossed Osaka Pass. Many among them were fashionably dressed ladies, not one of whom seemed to be making the pilgrimage with any thought of the hereafter. Each showed off her clothes and took such pride in her appearance that even Kannon must have been amused at the sight.

It happened that Osan and Moemon also made the pilgrimage together. They and the flowers they saw seemed to share a common fate: no one could tell when they might fall. Nor could anyone tell whether the lovers again might see this bay and the hills around Lake Biwa, so Moemon and Osan wanted to make it a day to remember. They rented a small boat in Seta and wished that their love would last as long as the

Long Bridge of that town,[8] though their pleasure might still be short lived. Floating along, the lovers made waves serve them as pillow and bed, and the disorder of Osan's hairdress testified to the nature of their delight. But there were moments, too, when the be-clouded Mirror Mountain seemed to reflect a more somber mood in Osan. Love for these two was as dangerous a passage as Crocodile Strait, and their hearts sank when at Katada someone called the boat from shore; for a minute they feared that a courier had come after them from Kyoto.

Even though they survived this, it seemed as if their end might be told by the snows of Mt. Hiei, for they were twenty years old and it is said that the snow on this Fuji-of-the-Capital always melts before twenty days have passed. So they wept and wet their sleeves and at the ancient capital of Shiga, which is now just a memory of past glory, they felt sadder still, thinking of their own inevitable end. When the dragon lanterns were lit, they went to Shirahige Shrine and prayed to the gods, now even more aware of the precariousness of their fate.

"After all, we may find that longer life only brings

[8] *Seta no Nagahashi*—built by Gyogi during the Nara period. This opens a passage studded with similar references, called a *michiyuki*, by which the characters' moods are described in terms of the places they visit on a journey.

They and the flowers they saw seemed to share a common
fate: no one could tell when they might fall. Nor could
anyone tell whether the lovers again might see this
bay and the hills around Lake Biwa....

greater grief," Osan told him. "Let us throw our-selves into the lake and consecrate our lives to Buddha in the Eternal Land."

But Moemon, though he valued his life hardly at all, was not so certain as to what would follow after death. "I think I have hit upon a way out," he said. "Let us each send letters to the capital, saying that we shall drown ourselves in the lake. We can then steal away from here, go anywhere you please, and pass the rest of our years together."

Osan was delighted. "When I left home, it was with that idea in mind. So I brought along five hun-dred pieces of gold in my suitcase."

That, indeed, was something with which to start life anew. "We must be careful how we do this," Moemon cautioned, as they set about writing notes to various people saying: "Driven by evil desires, we have joined in a sinful love which cannot escape Heaven's decree. Life has no place for us now; therefore today we depart forever from the Fleeting World."

Osan then removed the small image of the Buddha which she had worn as a charm for bodily protection, and trimmed the edges of her black hair. Moemon took off the great sword, which he wore at his side, made by Seki Izumi-no-Kami, with an iron guard em-bellished by twisting copper dragons. These things

would be left behind so that people could identify them
as belonging to Moemon and Osan. Then, as a final
precaution, they even left their coats and sandals at the
foot of a willow by the shore. And since there lived
at the lakeside men with a long tradition as experts
in fishing, who could leap from the rocks into the
water, Moemon secretly hired two of them and explained his plan. They readily agreed to keep a
rendezvous with the couple that evening.

When Moemon and Osan had prepared themselves
properly, they opened the bamboo door of the inn and
roused everyone by shouting: "For reasons known
only to ourselves we are about to end our lives!" They
then rushed away, and shortly, from the height of a
craggy rock, faint voices were heard saying the Nem-
butsu,[9] followed by the sound of two bodies striking
the water. Everyone wept and raised a great commotion over it.

But Moemon put Osan on his back and carried her
around the foot of the mountain, deep into the forest
to a desolate village, while the divers swam underwater
and emerged on the beach undetected.

Meantime, all around beat their hands and lamented
the tragedy. With help from people living along the

[9] A very common, short prayer—"Homage to Amida Buddha"—by
which believers in Amida expect to achieve salvation.

shore they made a search, but found nothing. Then, as dawn broke, more tears fell upon the discovery of the lovers' personal effects. These were wrapped up quickly and sent back to Kyoto.

Out of concern for what people would think, the families involved privately agreed to keep the matter to themselves. But in a world full of busy ears the news was bound to leak out, and all spring long it gave people something to gossip about. There was indeed no end to the mischief these two souls created.

4. *The teahouse which had not heard of gold pieces*

Hand in hand, Moemon and Osan trekked across the wilderness of Tamba. They had to make their own road through the stubborn underbrush. At last they climbed a high peak and, looking back whence they had come, reflected on the terrors of their journey. It was, to be sure, the lot they had chosen; still, there was little pleasure in living on in the role of the dead. They were lost souls, miserably lost, on a route that was not even marked by a woodsman's footprints. Osan stumbled feebly along, so wretched that she

seemed to be gasping for what might be her last breath,
and her face lost all its color. Moemon tried every
means to revive and sustain his beloved, even catching
spring water in a leaf as it dripped from the rocks.
But Osan had little strength left to draw on. Her
pulse beat more and more faintly; any minute might
be her last.

Moemon could offer nothing at all in the way of
medicine. He stood by helplessly to wait for Osan's
end, then suddenly bent near and whispered in her ear:
"Just a little further on we shall come to the village
of some people I know. There we can forget all our
misery, indulge our hearts' desire with pillows side
by side, and talk again of love!"

When she heard this, Osan felt better right away.
"How good that sounds! Oh, you are worth paying
for with one's life!"

A pitiful women indeed, whom lust alone could
arouse, Osan was carried by Moemon pickaback into
the fenced enclosure of a tiny village. Here was the
highway to the capital, and a road running along the
mountainside wide enough for two horses to pass each
other. Here too was a teahouse thatched with straw
and built up of cryptomeria branches woven together
A sign said "Finest Home-brew Here," but the rice
paste was many days old and dust had deprived it

"Just a little further on we shall come to the village.... There
we can forget all our misery, indulge our hearts'
desire with pillows side by side, and talk again
of love!"... Osan felt better right away....

of its whiteness. On a side counter were tea brushes, clay dolls, and dancing-drummer dolls—and reminiscent of Kyoto and therefore a tonic to the weary travelers, who rested there awhile.

Moemon and Osan enjoyed it so that, upon leaving, they offered the old innkeeper one piece of gold. But he scowled unappreciatively, like a cat that is shown an umbrella.[10]

"Please pay me for the tea," he demanded, and they were amused to think that less than fifteen miles from the capital there should be a village which had not yet heard of gold pieces.

Thence the lovers went to a place called Kayabara, where lived an aunt of Moemon's whom he had not heard from for many years—who might be dead for all he knew. Calling on her, Moemon spoke of their family past, and she welcomed him as one of her own. The rest of the evening, with chin in hand and tears in her eyes, the old woman talked of nothing but his father Mosuke; but when day broke she became suddenly aware of Osan, whose beauty and refinement aroused her suspicions.

"What sort of person is she?" his aunt asked.

Moemon had not prepared himself for all the questions she might ask and found himself in an awkward

---

[10] Equivalent to "casting pearls before swine."

spot. "My younger sister," he replied. "For many years she has served in the home of a court official, but it was a strict family and she disliked the fretful life of the capital. She thought there might be an opportunity to join a quiet, leisurely household—something like this—in the mountains. So she terminated her service and came along with me in hopes of finding housework and gardening to do in the village. Her expenses need be no concern; she has about two hundred gold pieces in savings."

Thus he blithely concocted a story to satisfy the old woman. But it is a greedy world wherever one goes, and Moemon's aunt thought there might be something in this for her.

"Now," she exclaimed, "that is really most fortunate. My son has no wife yet and your sister is a relative, so why not have her marry him?"[11]

It was a distressing proposal. Osan sobbed quietly, cursing the fate which had led her to such a dismal prospect.

Then as evening fell the son came home. He was frightful to behold, taller than anyone she had ever seen, and his head sat like a Chinese-lion gargoyle on his squat neck. A fierce light gleamed in his big, blood-

[11] Marriage between relatives once removed was not considered tabu. On the contrary, a match between cousins was thought to provide special intimacy.

shot eyes. His beard was like a bear's, his arms and
legs were as thick as pine trees, and a wisteria vine held
together the rag-woven clothes he wore. In one hand
he carried an old matchlock, in the other a tinder-rope.
His hunting basket was full of rabbits and badgers, as
much as to say: "This is how I make a living." He
was called Zetaro the Rock-jumper.

In the village it was no secret that he was a mean
man. But when his mother explained to him her proposal for a marriage with the lady from Kyoto, Zetaro
was pleased.

"Good, let's waste no time. Tonight will do." And
he reached for a hand mirror to look at his face. "Nice
looking fellow," he said.

His mother prepared the wedding cup, offered them
salted fish, and passed around a wine bottle which had
had its neck broken off. She used floor mats as screens
to enclose the room which would serve as the nuptial
chamber. Two wooden pillows were also provided,
two thin sleeping mats, and one striped bedcover.
Split pine logs burned in the brazier. It would be a
gay evening.

But Osan was as sad as could be, and Moemon was
terribly depressed.

"This is the price I must pay for having spoken so
impulsively. We are living on when we should have

died in the waters of Omi. Heaven will not spare us
now!" He drew his sword and would have killed himself had not Osan stopped and quieted him.

"Why, you are much too short-tempered. There are
still ways to get out of this. At dawn we shall depart
from here—leave everything to me."

That night while she was drinking the wedding cup
with good grace and affability, Osan remarked to
Zetaro: "Most people shun me. I was born in the
year of the Fiery Horse."[12]

"I wouldn't care if you were a Fiery Cat or a Fiery
Wolf. I even like blue lizards—eat 'em in fact. And
you see I'm not dead yet. Twenty-seven years old, and
I haven't had one case of worms. Mister Moemon
should take after me! As for you—a soft creature
brought up in the capital isn't what I'd like for a wife,
but I'll tolerate you since you're my relative." In this
generous mood he lay down and snuggled his head
comfortably in her lap.

Amidst all their unhappiness Osan and Moemon
found the brute somewhat amusing. Nevertheless,

[12] This year marked the coincidence of Fire with Fire in the old
unar calendar, the horse itself representing Fire. It was a dangerous
year to be born in, according to the old astrological interpretations,
and women born thus were said to bully and frequently kill their husbands. For this reason they had a hard time getting married. Zetaro's
reply is in the nature of a crude joke, for there is no year of the
Fiery Wolf and he speaks of it only as a symbol of frightfulness.

they could hardly wait until he went to bed, at last giving them a chance to slip away. Again they hid themselves in the depths of Tamba. Then after many days had passed they came out upon the road to Tango.

One night they slept in a chapel of the god Monju, who appeared to Osan in a dream midway through the night.

"You have committed the worst of sins. Wherever you go, you cannot escape its consequences. But that is all part of the unredeemable past; henceforth you must forsake your vain ways, shave off the hair you take such delight in, and become a nun. Once separated, the two of you can abandon your evil passion and enter upon the Way of Enlightenment. Then perhaps your lives may be saved!"

It was a worthy vision, but Osan heard herself answering: "Please don't worry about what becomes of us. We are more than glad to pay with our lives for this illicit affair. Monju may understand the love of men for men,[13] but he knows nothing about the love of women."

That instant she awoke from her dream, just as the morning breeze blew in through Hashidate's seaside pines, bearing with it the dust of the world.

[13] According to a vulgar belief, Manjusri (Monju in Japanese) was the lover of Shakyamuni Buddha. He was therefore taken as the patron god of homosexuals.

"Everything is dust and defilement," Osan told herself, and all hope was lost of ever saving her.

5. The eavesdropper whose ears were burned

Men take their misfortunes to heart and keep them there. A gambler does not talk about his losses; the frequenter of brothels, who finds his favorite engaged by another, pretends to be just as well off without her; the professional street-brawler is quiet about the fights he has lost; and a merchant who speculates in goods will conceal the losses he may suffer. They are all like the "man who steps on dog dung in the dark."

But of them all the one who has a wanton, mischievous wife will feel his misfortune most, convinced that there is no more heartless creature in the world than she. To the outer world Osan's husband treated her as a closed issue: she was dead, and nothing could be said or done about her. There were times when he was reminded of their years together and would feel the greatest bitterness toward Osan, yet he would still call in a priest to hold services in her memory. Ironically enough, he offered one of her choice silk garments as an altarcloth for the local temple, where, fluttering in the fickle wind of Life and Death, it became a further source of lamentation.

Even so, there is no one bolder than a man deeply attached to the things of this world, and Moemon, who before was so prudent that he never went outdoors at night, soon lost himself in a nostalgic desire to see the capital again. Dressing in the most humble attire and pulling his hat down over his eyes, he left Osan in the care of some villagers and made a senseless trip to Kyoto, all the while fearing more for his own safety than would a man who is about to deliver himself into the hands of an enemy.

It began to get dark when he reached the neighborhood of Hirozawa, and the sight of the moon, reflected as two in the pond, made him think again of Osan, so that his sleeve became soaked with idle tears. Presently he put behind him the rapids of Narutaki, with myriad bubbles dancing over the rocks, and hurried on toward Omuro and Kitano, for he knew that way well. When he entered the city his fears were multiplied. "What's that!" he would ask himself, when he saw his own silhouette under the waning moon, and his heart would freeze with terror.

In the quarter with which he was so familiar, because his former master lived there, he took up eavesdropping to learn the state of things. He heard about the inquiry which was to be made into the overdue payment from Edo, and about the latest styles in hair-dress, as discussed by a gathering of young men, who were also commenting on the style and fit of each others' clothes—the sort of silly chatter that love and lust inspire in men. When these topics of conversation were exhausted, sure enough they fell to talking about Moemon.

"That rascal Moemon, stealing a woman more beautiful than all the others! Even though he paid with his worthless life for it, he certainly got the best of the bargain—a memory worth dying with!"

But a man of more discernment upheld morality against Moemon. "He's nobody to raise up in public. He'd stink in the breeze. I can't imagine anyone worse than a man who'd cheat both his master and a husband at once."

Overhearing this, Moemon swore to himself: "That's the voice of the scoundrel Kisuke, of the Daimonji-ya. What a heartless, faithless fellow to be so outspoken against me. Why, I lent him eighty *momme* of silver on an IOU! But I'll get even for what he just said: I'll get that money back if I have to wring his neck."

Moemon gnashed his teeth and stood up in a rage. Still, there was nothing a man hiding from the world could do about the insults offered him, and while he suppressed his outraged feelings another man started to speak.

"Moemon's not dead. He's living with Mistress Osan somewhere around Ise, they say, having a wonderful time."

This shook Moemon and sent chills through his body. He left in all haste, took a room in a lodging-house along Third Avenue, and went to bed without even taking a bath. Since it was the night of the seventeenth,[14] he wrapped up twelve *mon* in a piece of paper and handed it to a beggar who would buy some candles and keep the vigil for him that night. Then he prayed that people would not discover who he was. But could he expect that even Atago-sama, the patron of lovers, would help him in his wickedness?

In the morning, as a last memory of the capital before leaving it, he stole down Higashi-yama to the theatre section at Shijo-gawara. Someone told him that it was the opening day of a three-act Kabuki drama featuring Fujita.

"I must see what it is like and tell Osan when I return."

[14] The Moon-Waiting Night *(Tsukimachi)*. It was the custom to spend the evening in prayer while waiting for the moonrise. Frequently a proxy was hired to keep the vigil in one's stead.

He rented a cushion and sat far back to watch from a distance, uneasy at heart lest someone recognize him. The play was about a man whose daughter was stolen away. It made Moemon's conscience hurt. Then he looked down to the front rows. There was Osan's husband. At the sight Moemon's spirit almost left him. He felt like a man with one foot dangling over hell, and the sweat stood like pearls on his forehead. Out he rushed through an exit to return to the village of Tango, which he did not think of leaving again for Kyoto.

At that time, when the Chrysanthemum Festival was almost at hand, a chestnut peddler made his annual trip to the capital. While speaking of one thing and another at the house of the almanac maker, he asked where the mistress was, but as this was an awkward subject in the household none of the servants ventured to answer.

Frowning, Osan's husband told him: "She's dead."

"That's strange," the peddler went on. "I've seen someone who looks very much like her, in fact, someone who doesn't differ from her one particle. And with her is the living image of your young man. They are near Kirito in Tango."

When the peddler had departed, Osan's husband sent someone to check up on what he had heard.

Learning that Osan and Moemon were indeed alive, he gathered together a good number of his own people, who went and arrested them.

There was no room for mercy in view of their crime. When the judicial inquiry was duly concluded, the lovers, together with a maidservant named Tama who had been their go-between earlier, were paraded as an example before the crowds along the way to Awada-guchi, where they died like dewdrops falling from a blade of grass.

Thus they met their end on the morning of September twenty-second, with, it should be remarked, a touching acquiescence in their fate. Their story spread everywhere, and today the name of Osan still brings to mind her beautiful figure, clothed in the pale-blue slip which she wore to her execution.

1. A dark New Year's for new lovers

A fierce winter wind blew in from the northeast and clouds moved with swift feet through the December sky. Around a *mochi*-maker's[1] shop, bustling with preparations for New Year's, a man was sweeping with a small bamboo broom in each hand. The store scales gleamed, polished only by frequent use as the arbiters of all trade. Children ran under the jutting shop-roofs and made a merry racket with their cries of "Kon, kon, a penny please for the little blind fox."[2] Old signs were being torn down. The streets were full of peddlers selling firewood, pine nuts, dried chestnuts, and giant lobsters. In a side lane, toy bows and arrows

[1] *Mochi*—rice paste in the form of a dumpling.
[2] Children blindfold themselves and pretend to be little foxes, just as American children go begging at Halloween in the guise of witches, ghosts, etc. The fox's voice was thought to change in December so that it sounded something like "Kon, kon."

could be seen in an open stall, and farther along a new stock of snow-clogs and socks was hung on display, "feet in the air," as Kenko said.[3] This was indeed a season which gave tradesmen no rest.

It was close to the end of the year, at midnight on the twenty-eighth, when some houses caught fire and great panic arose. Heavy chests, creaking on their rollers, were pulled out of burning buildings. Men slung wicker baskets and big inkstands[4] on their backs and took them away, while lighter household articles were thrown under the lids of deep storage-holes. In a moment everything else went up in smoke. And as the pheasant in a field afire thinks first of its young, so the victims of this disaster anxiously called their loved ones who had been scattered in the confusion. Then, grief-stricken, they went to the homes of friends.

In the Hongo section of Edo lived a greengrocer named Hachibei, whose ancestors had been of some quality and who had an only daughter named Oshichi,

[3] From a passage in the *Tsurezure-Gusa* describing a popular custom on the last night of the year, when people went around with pinewood flares, knocking on doors, shouting noisily, and "scurrying about with their feet in the air" (as if flying). By this allusion Saikaku suggests the atmosphere of a roisterous and prankish New Year's Eve.

[4] These were big enough to hold drawers in which family valuables were kept, and so were among the first objects to be rescued in the event of fire.

fifteen years old, as beautiful as the blossoms of Ueno, as delicately radiant as the moon shining on Sumidagawa. Indeed, it was unfortunate that she had not appeared in the time of Narihira, for the *miyako* bird[5] could not have found a lady so fair. In her own time Oshichi was the woman of almost every man's desire.

As the flames approached their dwelling that night, Oshichi's mother took her to a local temple, the Kichijo-ji in Komagome, where they had been regular communicants for many years. In their plight the two took refuge there. And they were not the only ones to do so. The superior's rooms were filled by the cries of a newborn babe, and a woman had spread her underclothing before the image of Buddha. Wives were stepping over their husbands,[6] sleepers made pillows of their relatives, and everyone slept in careless disorder. In the morning a bowl-shaped container for the temple gong was converted into a washbasin, and big teacups were used as makeshift rice bowls. Yet Buddha himself could not but look indulgently upon all this, knowing how it had come to pass.

Her mother kept a careful eye on Oshichi. "It's

[5] Refers to a poem by the famous ninth-century lover Narihira, who, exiled to this region, longed for his lady in the capital *(miyako)* and asked the *miyako* bird to bring him tidings of her.

[6] Considered a very disrespectful thing for a wife to do.

a tricky world," she said, "even among priests," and she was not going to take any chances.

Then it happened one night that a terrible storm came up, which the refugees were in no condition to withstand. Out of pity for them the monk who was responsible for their care lent out whatever extra clothing he had. There was one garment of soft, black silk, with low-hanging sleeves, a crest of a paired paulownia leaf and an almond flower, and a red lining which trailed around the skirt like a path around a mountain. Its design seemed to Oshichi to have some special significance, which was enhanced by a lingering odor of incense.

"What fine lady fled from the world, leaving this souvenir of her unhappiness so sad to behold? Perhaps she was just my age—how unfortunate that would have been! I did not know her, but surely her fate is the fate of all. Life is a dream in which nothing has value, and only the awakening, the life hereafter, is real."

In this somber mood Oshichi opened her mother's rosary bag and took the beads in her hands. Over and over she repeated the prayer of homage to the Lotus. But while doing so she noticed an attractive samurai youth with a pair of silver tweezers in one hand, trying to remove a splinter that seemed to have stuck in the index finger of his left hand. He had slid back the paper door-screen and was struggling in the twilight to remove the splinter.

Oshichi's mother, unable to bear the sight of him in such difficulty, told the young man to come and let her take the splinter out. She took the tweezers and did her best for a while, but, being an old woman, her eyesight was none too good. She could not find the splinter.

Seeing how much trouble they were having, Oshichi thought perhaps a pair of young, strong eyes was needed to extract the splinter. Nevertheless, modesty kept her from going up to help.

At last, to her delight, Mother suggested that Oshichi try. Taking the tweezers, she soon delivered him from pain, but by this time the young man's thoughts were entirely of his deliverer and not at all of the splinter. Impulsively he squeezed her hand tight. He did not want Oshichi to go any more than she herself did, but Mother was watching and, like it or not, they had to part.

Oshichi started away, intentionally keeping the tweezers in her hand. "Oh, I must take these back," she said to her mother a moment later, and following after the young man, she squeezed his hand as he had hers. Then he knew that she shared his feelings.

...*an attractive samurai youth with a pair of silver tweezers in one hand, trying to remove a splinter....Seeing how much trouble they were having, Oshichi thought perhaps a pair of young, strong eyes was needed....*

As time went by Oshichi took a deep fancy to him. "What sort of person is that young man?" she asked the monk in charge of the refectory one day.

"He is Sir Onogawa Kichisaburo, a man of fine ancestry and a knight without a lord. He is a gentle, sensitive sort of person."

Now this made Oshichi think still more of Kichisaburo. Time and again she wrote notes to him and had them delivered in secret. Then at last someone came with an answer, and thereafter, as one earnest note followed upon another, desire fed upon desire until they fell in love with all their hearts. But love letters alone were not enough. Until the time came for them to meet, to love and be loved, it would be a dreary world for them indeed.

On New Year's Eve the sun sank lovesick into the night and rose again, a shining jewel, upon the sparkling New Year. Festive pines stood together like lovers, symbols perhaps for the second day of the new calendar when men could have their girls again. But there was no satisfaction in all this for the new lovers, who still slept apart. Then came the day to gather young herbs for broth and drink to the health of one's husband. When it was over, the days passed—the ninth, tenth, eleventh, twelfth, and thirteenth—until the evening of the fourteenth arrived and the pine boughs were taken away, bringing the celebration to an end. Empty, useless days they had been, holidays in name only for lovers who had no way to celebrate.

2. Spring thunder shakes out someone in summer underwear

From Yanagiwara, where spring rain had strung the willows with pearls, a man came knocking on the temple gate the night of the fifteenth, and roused the monks from sleep. "The rice dealer Hachizaemon, who has been ill a long time, passed away this evening. His family was expecting him to die and they want to take his body to the graveyard tonight."

It was a job that required the services of priests, so a large number of them prepared to officiate at the funeral. They did not wait for the sky to clear, but took up umbrellas and set out directly, leaving at the temple only a kitchen cook, seventy or more years old, an eleven- or twelve-year-old novice, and a red-haired dog. These, and the others who had taken refuge at the temple, listened to the mourning of the wind in the pines and were terrified at the crashes of thunder, which shook worms from the ground. The aged cook brought out some fried beans which had been used at New Year's to drive away evil spirits, and then hid herself in the attic.

Oshichi's mother was distraught with fears for her daughter. "Take care of yourself," she urged Oshichi. "Get under your covers and, when the thunder breaks, cover up your ears." They were women after all, and women will do most anything when frightened.

Oshichi, however, thought what a good time this would be to see Kichisaburo. "Tonight or never," she resolved, and to the others she said: "Why should we here be frightened by a little thunder? I was ready to die in the fire. I am not going to fear for my life now."

The serving-women who heard her took this as mere bluster, coming from a girl who could really be no braver than other women, and they criticized Oshichi for it.

By and by, as it grew later, everyone went to bed, and the patter of rain on the roof could hardly be heard above their snoring. When all was still and moonlight broke fitfully through the cracks in the storm doors, Oshichi stole out of the guestchamber, not too steady on her feet nor too sure of her footing. Suddenly her foot struck the behind of someone sprawled out in sleep.

Scared almost out of her wits, Oshichi felt as if she were going to faint. She could say nothing, merely joining her hands in the attitude of prayer, until it struck her as strange that the sleeper did not yell or make a fuss.

Collecting her courage, Oshichi took a good look—it was the maidservant named Mume, who worked in the kitchen.

As Oshichi stepped over her, the maid suddenly reached up and pulled at Oshichi's skirt, frightening her all over again.

"Is she stopping me?" Oshichi wondered. No, it was not that. The maid just held up some tissues of paper for her.

Oshichi took the paper, both relieved and amused. "Well, she certainly knows what goes on at night, and she has a ready wit for awkward moments."

Oshichi then proceeded to the priests' quarters but was unable to find her lover asleep there. Disappointed, she wandered down to the kitchen, where the cook was awake, muttering to herself: "The cursed rats are out tonight." In one hand she carried some mushroom stew, in the other fried bean-cakes and a bag of powdered bean-curds. As she was putting these things away, the cook noticed Oshichi.

"Kichisaburo's bedroom is the small one in which

the novice sleeps," she said frankly and patted Oshichi affectionately on the back.

Never having expected so much unsolicited sympathy, Oshichi loved the old woman for it. "She's too nice for a temple," she thought, as she undid her fawn-spotted sash and followed in the direction the cook had pointed out.

It must have been about the eighth hour, for the bell which served as a reminder of the perpetual incense burner fell with a ring that sounded throughout the temple for some time. Apparently the novice was supposed to be on duty. He got up, put the bell back on a string, and threw fresh incense on the fire. Then he sat at the altar for what seemed an eternity to Oshichi, who was impatient to enter the bedchamber. Acting on a sudden inspiration, as women are wont to do, she pulled down her hair, made a dreadful face, and approached the novice menacingly. But, imbued with the calm courage of Buddha, the novice was not the least bit frightened by her.

"You must be a wild women indeed, to parade around with your sash off. If you want to be the temple queen, wait until the priests come back. Now go away," he ordered with a stern and fearless look in his eyes.

Oshichi was somewhat taken aback but kept coming

towards him. "I just wanted you to take me to bed with you."

The novice laughed. "You mean Kichisaburo, don't you? We have been sleeping together, back to back," he said and held up his sleeve as evidence of it. On his sleeve lingered the fragrant odor of incense, which Oshichi recognized as that made from the white chrysanthemum.

"Don't! I can't stand it any longer," she sighed and made her way toward the bedchamber.

"Hey, Oshichi has come to have a good time," the novice called out ahead of her.

Alarmed, Oshichi begged him to be quiet. "Whatever you want most I promise to buy for you."

"Well, in that case, I guess there is nothing I'd like better than eighty *sen* in cash, a pack of Matsuba-ya playing cards, and five pieces of *manju* candy from Asakusa."

"Those will be easy to get. I'll send for them the first thing in the morning," she promised.

The novice went to bed and fell asleep telling himself: "I will get those three things in the morning. I'll get them for sure."

Thereafter Oshichi was free to indulge her desires. She went over to the sleeping Kichisaburo and lay down voluptuously beside him.

He got up, put the bell back on a string, and threw fresh incense on the fire. Then he sat at the altar for what seemed an eternity to Oshichi, who was impatient to enter the bedchamber....

He awoke with a start, as Oshichi pulled back the bedclothing, which he had drawn up over his head.

"You shouldn't let your hair get mussed that way," she teased.

"I'm just fifteen," he replied in distress.

"I'm just fifteen myself," she said.

"But I'm so afraid of the superior," Kichisaburo insisted.

"I'm afraid of him too."

Love-making was indeed slow and awkward at the start. Together at last, they found themselves weeping in confusion and embarrassment. But suddenly the rain let up and a great clash of thunder sounded in the night.

"Oh, how frightening!" Oshichi exclaimed and held tight to Kichisaburo, whereupon love began to take its natural course.

"Your hands and feet are so cold," Kichisaburo said, bringing her closer still.

Oshichi pouted. "You seemed to like me well enough when you sent me those passionate letters. Whose fault is it if my body has grown cold?" Then she bit him on the neck and in a moment they were in the throes of love.

Afterward, covering each other with their sleeves to

keep warm in their dampness, they resolved to be in love like this forever. But soon day broke. The bell of Yanaka rang busily and a strong breeze blew in through the nettle treees of Fukuage.

"It is so annoying. We have hardly had time to warm up the bed and must part already. The world is wide enough—there should be one land where night lasts throughout the day."

It was a futile hope, and it gave them no consolation at all when Oshichi's mother suddenly appeared, looking for the daughter, who was missing from her bed. As she pulled Oshichi away, Kichisaburo was lost in confusion and despair, as heartbroken as the lover of old, Narihira, had been when a demon's menacing jaws frightened his sweetheart away from him one rainy night.

The novice, however, had not forgotten Oshichi's promise last evening. "If you don't give me those three things now, I'll tell everybody what happened last night."

The mother stopped a moment. "I don't know what you are talking about, but if Oshichi promised you anything, I will see that you get it." And then she went away.

A mother with a wanton daughter does not have to be told the whole story to get the point. She was even more concerned than Oshichi about the danger of scandal and, first thing that morning, went out shopping to get the novice his baubles.

3. *A nice place to stay on a snowy night*

In this world we cannot afford to be careless. When traveling, keep the money in your waistband out of sight. Do not display your knife to a drunkard, and don't show your daughter to a monk, even if he seems to have given up the world.

Oshichi's mother had this in mind when she took her daughter home from the temple, tearing the lovers apart and adding to their unhappiness. But through the kindness of a maid they were able to write to each other frequently, and so to share at least their mutual yearnings. Then one night a country boy, apparently from somewhere near Itabashi, came along with a basketful of truffles and "horsetails," which he sold for a living. Oshichi called him in to buy some for her mother. It was snowing that night, although it was spring, and the boy did not look forward to his long trip home. So the master took pity on him. Without

...and don't show your daughter to a monk, even if he seems to have given up the world. Oshichi's mother had this in mind when she took her daughter home from the temple, tearing the lovers apart....

a thought for what it might mean, he told him to
spend the night in a corner of the courtyard and return
home in the morning.

The boy proceeded to clear a straw mat of the
radishes and burdocks spread upon it. Covering his
head with his bamboo rainhat and his body with the
bottom half of his straw raincoat, he lay down to pass
the night there. But the wind blew hard around his
sleeping place, and the earthen floor gave him chills,
It was not at all a healthy place to lie in. Before long
he was wheezing and gasping, and his eyes grew
bleary.

When Oshichi noticed this, she called out: "The
country boy, poor thing—give him something to drink,
hot water if nothing else!"

So Mume, the kitchenmaid, put hot water in a
kitchen cup and gave it to a manservant, Kyushichi,
who took the cup to the boy.

"It's very kind of you," the grateful lad said.

"You should live in Edo," Kyushichi cooed, stroking
the boy's forelock in the darkness. "You would have
so many admirers here. It's really too bad. . . ."

"But I was brought up in such rude style. I don't
know about anything except woodcutting or leading
a plow horse."

Kyushichi fondled the boy's feet. "It's nice they

aren't all chapped and cracked. Now how about your mouth?"

As Kyushichi bent forward the boy clenched his teeth and tears filled his eyes, so distasteful was all this to him. But Kyushichi had sense enough not to persist. "Ugh, your mouth smells of garlic or leeks or something." And with this excuse he gave up his obnoxious advances.

It was soon bedtime for the rest of the household. By dim lamplight the servants climbed upstairs on a ladder nailed to the wall. The master saw to it that his safe was locked.

"Take care with your lamp fires," his wife cautioned everyone, and then, ever mindful of her daughter, she slid shut the door to the girl's room. No lover would pass that way tonight.

The midnight bell had just rung when someone knocked on the outer door. A man and woman were heard calling: "Nursey just came in for the blessed event! It's a boy and the father is overjoyed!"

Their cries caused a stir in the house. "How wonderful!" exclaimed Oshichi's father and mother as they came running from their bedroom. Quickly they picked up some seaweed and licorice,[7] told Oshichi

[7] For mixing into a laxative syrup which was thought to cleanse newborn infants of impurities left in them from the womb.

to close the door behind them, and rushed from the house, each in his haste wearing but one slipper.

Oshichi closed the door and had started back to bed when she thought of the country boy. "Carry a candle for me," she told one of the maids, and went out to see him.

How forlorn the boy looked, sprawled out there on the earthen floor!

"He's comfortable enough," observed the maid. "Don't disturb him."

But Oshichi pretended not to hear and went near enough so that she could smell the fragrance of a Hyobukyo sachet[8] he was wearing. Pulling back his raincoat, she stood there entranced by the sight of his rumpled hair and of his face, barely visible.

"I wonder how old he is," she thought, poking a hand into his garments to find that he was wearing underwear of fine, yellow silk.

"What's this!" she cried in amazement.

It was Kichisaburo.

"Why in the world do you come looking like this?" Oshichi asked aloud, without a thought of being overheard, and clasped him tenderly.

Confronted by her so suddenly, Kichisaburo was

[8] Named after the son of Genji, Kaoru ("Fragrant"), who was known by his title, Minister of Military Affairs (*Hyobukyo*).

speechless for a moment. "I disguised myself like this
in the hope of seeing you for just a little while. Please
understand: I have suffered so much for you tonight."
He began to tell her all the things that had happened
to him, one after the other.

"Well, come inside first. Then you can tell me
all your troubles," she said, taking his hand to lead
him in.

But Kichisaburo's suffering that evening left him too
weak to walk, so Oshichi and the maid put their hands
together, making a cradle in which to carry him. They
proceeded to one of the bedrooms, gave his hands as
hard a rubbing as they could stand, and brought him
so many different kinds of medicine that he could not
help smiling a little.

"We shall drink the cup of love together and spend
the night emptying our hearts to each other."

Just then, alas, her father came home, and misfortune seemed to be upon them again. Kichisaburo
hid himslf behind a clothes rack, expecting any moment to be discovered. But nothing happened.

"Well," Oshichi greeted her father, "are both Ohatsu
and the boy doing well?"

"Yes, thank goodness!" the happy old man answered. "She is my only niece and I couldn't help
being anxious about her. It's a load off my mind."

*...she could smell the fragrance of a Hyobukyo sachet he
was wearing. Pulling back his raincoat, she stood
there entranced by the sight of his rumpled
hair and of his face, barely visible....*

Then in his exuberance he started planning for the baby's layette.

"Everything will be festive, all the lucky things—storks and turtles, pine and bamboo—in decorative designs with silver and gold powder sprinkled on the cloth. . . ."

"But," one of the maids suggested, "there is no great hurry about it, sir. You can do it at your leisure tomorrow."

"No, no, the sooner you do such things the better," he insisted. He took some paper from a pillow drawer, spread it out, and began to cut out patterns. Everyone else was annoyed, and after some time the maids at last coaxed him into going to bed.

Then the lovers would have liked to talk together, but as there was only one thin screen enclosing them, they were afraid of being overheard. So they got out ink and paper and in the lamplight wrote down everything on their minds and in their hearts. Showing their notes to each other, they made love as silently as the mandarin ducks painted on the screen behind them.

Thus throughout the night their touching correspondence went on.

When dawn came to separate them, their longing for each other was unappeased. It was a sad life,

not as they would have it, and they might not meet
again.

4. *Farewell to the cherry blossom*

Night and day poor Oshichi was sick at heart but
said nothing about it to anyone. She did not know
when she would see her lover again. Then one stormy
night she recalled the great conflagration from which
she had sought refuge in the temple, and it struck her
that another such disturbance might give her a chance
to see Kichisaburo. Mad as it was, this desire prompted
her to commit a crime which proved her undoing.
She started a fire, but the first traces of smoke aroused
people's curiosity. When they looked in to investigate,
they found Oshichi there on the spot.

Apprehended and questioned, she told her whole
story without any attempt to conceal the truth, and
it soon became known to all as the most tragic story
of the time. That very day Oshichi was exposed to
shame on the old bridge of Kanda, and later at Yotsuya,
Asakusa, Shiba, and Nihombashi. Everywhere people
gathered around to look and there was no one who

did not pity her. Nor could anyone who thought about the case fail to see that crime must always be avoided. Heaven does not tolerate it.

Since the girl felt no remorse, however, her person did not waste away. Each day she looked just as she always had. Each day her black hair was nicely dressed and her figure was lovelier than ever. Alas, she was only sixteen, but even the flowers of spring must one day lose their petals and die, while the ardent cuckoo joins in general lamentation: "This is the end, this is the end."

Still firmly resigned, Oshichi told herself, "It is all a dream, an illusion," and she relied upon a prayer to Amida for salvation. In her hand she held a sprig of late-blooming cherry, a token of someone's deep sympathy for her.

Gazing at it, she sang: "How sad a world it is, when I must fall today like the last blossoms of the cherry and leave my ill fame to blow about in the winds of spring."

Her song redoubled the grief of those who stood by until she was put to death, which was soon to come as it must sometime to every living thing. At dawn the bell struck, and in the roadside grasses, no longer green, Oshichi gave up her life to join the wisps of smoke that hovered in the morning air. Death, the

Night and day poor Oshichi was sick at heart but said nothing about it to anyone. She did not know when she would see her lover again. . . . Mad as it was, this desire prompted her to commit a crime which proved her undoing. . . .

smoke of life, lies waiting at the end of every road. Nothing is so certain, nothing so sad.

But that was yesterday. Today in Suzu-no-Mori the ashes and dust are gone and only the wind-blown pines remain. The travelers who pass that way have all heard the story of Oshichi. None of them goes on before he has made an offering in her memory. On the day of her death even the shreds of Oshichi's underwear were picked up by people and saved, to become the inspiration for countless stories in later times. And even those who did not know her well came to plant anise by her grave on days of mourning.

To some inquisitive souls, however, it seemed strange that Oshichi's lover had not tried to follow her in death. So they started ugly rumors about him, little knowing that he was still unaware of her death and still so madly in love with her that he could not tell front from back. Indeed, he seemed on the verge of death himself, with little to live for, half out of his mind. His friends were so concerned that they asked each other: "If we tell him the news of Oshichi, what chance is there he will live?"

Meanwhile Kichisaburo decided to put his affairs in order and await the end, for death could not be far off. But his friends, trying to keep hope alive by telling him nice things, said: "Today or tomorrow she will come, looking just exactly as you remember her."

At this his spirits revived. He refused to take the medicines they brought him and began to talk as if in a dream. "Dearest, I love you!" he cried out, and then called in despair: "Has she not come yet?"

Thus he mourned, unwittingly, on the fifth day of mourning[9] since her death five weeks before. On the seventh day of mourning, when *mochi* was prepared for all close relatives, Oshichi's parents went to the temple and begged that they be allowed to see her lover. It was explained to them what a state he was in.

"This might bring on another tragedy," his friends argued, until the parents agreed to leave things as they stood.

"If he is a man at all, he could never live on after hearing the news. We shall keep it a deep secret until his illness has passed and he is well again. Then we can tell him Oshichi's last words that day and cherish him as a reminder of her."

Consoling themselves in this way, the parents had a gravestone set up and inscribed to Oshichi. On it they sprinkled memorial water, which with their tears kept the stone ever moist. In shape the gravestone somehow resembled Oshichi, or so it seemed to the

[9] Every seventh day, for seven weeks after death, was a day of mourning.

weeping eyes of her mother. Such is the unpredict-
ability of life in this topsy-turvy world, that the mother
should be left behind to mourn the untimely death
of her daughter.

5. The sudden decision to become a monk

Fate is unreliable, but there is nothing so inexorable.

"If I died," Kichisaburo thought, "both my love
and all this bitterness would come to an end."

It was one hundred days after Oshichi's death when
the young man arose from his bed and, leaning on a
bamboo staff, went for his first walk in the quiet
precincts of the temple. There was a new gravestone,
he noticed, and what a shock it was to see the name
upon it!

"Alas, that I should not have been told! People
will not understand this. They will say that cowardice
made me slow to follow her. The gossip will be
unbearable."

He reached for his sword, but the monks caught him
in time.

"Your life may not be worth living, but there is

your sworn friend[10] to take leave of, and the superior, who must be told what you have in mind. Ask him to decide your fate. The fact is, it was your sworn brother who left you in the care of this temple out of consideration for his vow to cherish and watch over you. Now you must consider the unhappiness it would bring to him. Above all, you must not be the cause of further tragedy."

So they remonstrated with him, and their arguments proved convincing. He gave up his idea of suicide. Still, he had no real desire to go on living in the world, and told the superior so, much to the latter's alarm.

"Your life is solemnly pledged to another, who earnestly besought us to look after you. He has now gone to Matsumae, but I hear that he is certain to come here this fall. Then you can explain everything to him. If anything happens before that time, it will be my fault and I will suffer for it. But as soon as he returns, you are free to do what you please."

Such was the advice of the superior, and since the young man was indebted to him for his recent kindness, he could only promise to do what the old priest

[10] There was a practice deriving from medieval times by which an older man exchanged a vow of lasting love with a younger one. It was generally a homosexual relationship, the elder "brother" promising to cherish and protect the younger in return for the latter's obedience and love. When Kichisaburo fell in love with Oshichi he was breaking his earlier pledge of faithfulness to the "elder brother."

"...People will not understand this. They will say that
cowardice made me slow to follow her. The gossip
will be unbearable." He reached for his sword,
but the monks caught him in time....

asked. Even so, for the sake of his own peace of mind, the superior took away Kichisaburo's sword, among other things, and assigned several men to keep a close watch on him. Thus nothing untoward happened until one day the young man came into the monks' quarters and began talking to them.

"I am alive, it is true, but I must suffer the most insufferable slander from everyone. Alas that I should still have been pledged to another, when that girl came along and made me a slave to her desires. To him I brought suffering, to her the worst misfortune. Now I am deserted by all, by the Buddha and by the gods who sanctified our oath of manly love. And the worst of it," he sobbed with deep emotion, "is what will happen when my sworn brother comes back. There is no way to justify myself before him. I must end my life quickly, before he returns. But people would call it unmanly for me to bite off my tongue or strangle myself. For pity's sake, give me my sword. What good will it do me to go on living?"

So he spoke in tears, and the gathering of monks was deeply moved and wet their sleeves with weeping. When Oshichi's parents heard of it, they came and spoke to him.

"We know your grief to be sincere, but Oshichi said many times when she died: 'If Kichisaburo loves me truly, he will abandon the world and become a monk of some kind. That way he can look after me when I am gone, and I shall never forget him, come what may. Even in the next world our love will not die.'"

When these words of hers still did not persuade him and he seemed determined to bite off his tongue, the mother bent near to whisper something in his ear. What she said no one else knows, but after listening to her for a while, Kichisaburo nodded his head.

At last his sworn brother returned and gave his young friend much sound advice, as a result of which Kichisaburo joined the priesthood. How sad it was to see his forelock shaven! The monk who had to do it threw his razor away. It was like a sudden storm destroying the flower in full bloom. Alive though he was, Kichisaburo seemed to suffer a fate worse than Oshichi's. People said of him that he was the prettiest priest of all time, and everyone thought it very sad.

But those whom love drives to the priesthood are good and true to their vows. The man who had been a sworn brother to Kichisaburo took the black-dyed robes himself when he returned to his old home in Matsumae.

And so this tale is told, with all its love and sadness, to show how unreal and uncertain life is, how much like a wild, fantastic dream.

Book Five

Gengobei, the
Mountain
of Love

1. The flute-playing ends on a sad note

There was a man named Gengobei who is still known to the world in popular songs. He was from Kagoshima in Satsuma Province and had a remarkable appetite for love considering that he came from such a remote and backward region. He wore his hair according to the fashion of his native place, down in back with a short tuft sticking up. His sword was quite long and conspicuous, but since this too was customary in his home province, people looked tolerantly upon it. Night and day he devoted himself to the love of young men. Not once in his life had he amused himself with the fragile, long-haired sex.

At this time Gengobei was twenty-five. For many years he had bestowed his favors upon a young boy, Nakamura Hachijuro, with whom he had fallen desperately in love at first sight and to whom he had pledged himself forever. Hachijuro was incomparably beautiful, resembling, one might say, the first bud of the cherry blossom with its petals half-open—a delicate flower of love.

One night it was raining drearily and the two men closed themselves up, all alone, in a small room where Gengobei used to stay. As they played the flute together and listened to the noises outside, the wistful beauty of the night captivated them. Through the window came stormy gusts of wind, bearing with them the fragrance of plum trees, which lingered on in the lovers' long, low-hanging sleeves. It was most touching of all to hear the sudden rustling of the bamboos, a sound which startled the nestling birds and set them aflutter.

Gradually the lamplight grew faint; the notes of the flute died away. Hachijuro, more appealing than ever, became more affectionate as they talked together happily. Every word spoken was charged with a love that sought expression in every possible way. Gengobei was overcome with the delightfulness of it and wished that Hachijuro might remain forever unchanged, always a boy with his forelock uncropped, which was an impossible desire, too foolish even for the world of folly.

Dawn approached as they lay together amidst the

disorder of their bed, and Gengobei dozed off to sleep. Hachijuro pinched himself to keep awake.

"How can you waste the precious night in dreams!" he exclaimed to the sleeper, who only half-heard the words and found them hard to comprehend. "This may be the last night for you to talk to me. Can't you think of something to say, some last words of farewell?"

Gengobei was startled and hurt. "You wound me with your playful talk. If someday we are kept apart, your face will haunt my dreams forever. What need is there to talk so foolishly, to say that tonight may be the end—just to get me stirred up!"

They took each other's hands and Hachijuro smiled weakly. "There is nothing sure about this Floating World. Who then can tell when life may come to an end?"

No sooner had he said this than his pulse failed. The parting he feared had become a reality.

"What's this!" Gengobei cried, and as the first shock gave way to uncontrolled grief, he wept and carried on in a terrible way until everyone came in to see what was the matter.

They gave Hachijuro medicines of all sorts, but to no avail. It was all over.

When Hachijuro's parents were told about this, their

*...and the two men closed themselves up, all alone, in a small
room.... As they played the flute together and listened
to the noises outside, the wistful beauty
of the night captivated them....*

grief knew no bounds. But they had known Gengobei well for many years and had no suspicions concerning Hachijuro's death.

All the boy's belongings—whatever they could find —were gotten together and sent to the graveyard. They stuffed his body just as it was into a large jar, which was buried in the shade of tall grasses growing by the roadside.

Gengobei prostrated himself on the mound, mourning his lost lover and wishing only that he himself could leave the world. "Alas, you were a frail one, were you not? I shall mourn for you just three years. Then, on this same day three years from now, I shall come here and join you among the ghosts."

So saying, he left the graveyard and quickly cut off his hair. He told his whole story from beginning to end to the superior of a temple known as Saien-ji, after which he devoted himself wholeheartedly to the priesthood.

In summertime he picked flowers each day and kept incense burning at the boy's grave. By and by, as the days passed with Gengobei deep in prayer for the salvation of Hachijuro, autumn arrived. Morning-glories soon were blooming on the hedges, their blossoms still another reminder of the awesome, unstable beauty of life.

"Even the dew outlasts men's lives," Gengobei thought, reflecting on the past, now lost forever. It was the eve of the Bon Festival, when a welcome was to be prepared for the returning souls of the dead. Gengobei cut some lavender and spread it on the floor, adding cucumbers and eggplant to his quaint display, with green soybeans scattered here and there. In the dim light of a hanging lantern he busily recited sutras before the altar of the dead, while hemp-sticks burned away in the fire of welcome for the ghosts.

But the evening of the fourteenth was not to be a quiet one even at the temple. Creditors stood outside clamoring for the money which monks owed to them,[1] and at the front gate a dancing drummer filled the air with his pounding.

"Here, too, life is becoming unpleasant," Gengobei thought, and so he decided to make a trip to Mt. Koya.[2]

In the morning, on the fifteenth day of the Poem Month,[3] he set out from his native place with his black

[1] All debts were to be repaid on this date, and monks were not immune to the claims of creditors.

[2] Site of a monastery founded in the ninth century by the great patriarch Kobo Daishi. It ranked with Mt. Hiei as the most important of Buddhist centers.

[3] The seventh month of the lunar calendar, so called because at this time of year came the Tanabata Festival, when women and girls wrote love poems to the Celestial Shepherd (Vega, the Weaver).

robes stained by tears and his sleeves worn thin from rubbing swollen eyes.

2. *A birdcatcher's life is as short as the bird's*

The village was getting ready for winter. Firewood was being cut and stacked, snow fences were being put up to hold back the first snowfall, and people were boarding up their northern windows, while all about there was a noisy beating of clothes. Gengobei went through the open fields and was watching some little birds fight for a nesting place in the red-leaved trees, when he noticed a boy of fourteen or fifteen—certainly not yet sixteen—dressed in a hempen gown with pale-blue lining and a violet sash of medium width. At his side he carried a sword with a gilded guard. His hair was swept up in tufts like little tea-brushes, and he had all the charm of a girl. Holding a bamboo pole at the middle, the boy aimed at one bird after another and threw his pole at least a hundred times without catching a single bird, much to his disappointment.

"I would never have believed that such a beautiful boy could be found in this world," said Gengobei, watching him. "At most he is no older than Hachijuro was, and for good looks he surpasses him by far."

All thought of death and the hereafter were quickly driven from his mind, and he stood and gazed till dusk. Finally he went up to the boy.

"I am a priest, but I still know how to catch birds. Let me have your pole," he said, baring his right arm for action.

"Ho, all you birds up there! What is so bad about dying in his lovely hands? Have you no appreciation for the company of young boys, you rascals?" In no time at all he brought down countless birds and the young fellow was overjoyed.

"How in the world did you happen to become a priest?" he inquired.

Gengobei told the whole story from beginning to end, losing himself in sad memories so that it brought tears to the eyes of the boy.

"How admirable of you," he exclaimed in sympathy and awe, "to take up the religious life for such a reason! You must by all means come home with me and spend the night under our roof."

The two of them were already fast friends as they walked together to his home, a charming place in the middle of the woods, built in the style of an imperial pavilion. Whinnying horses and armor which hung

..the boy...threw his pole at least a hundred times without
catching a single bird...."I would never have believed
that such a beautiful boy could be found in the
world," said Gengobei, watching him....

decoratively on the walls told Gengobei that this was the home of a samurai. He crossed a spacious hall and from the veranda could see steps leading away over a little bridge. There in a grove of striped bamboo was a garden bird-cage. He could hear wild geese, Chinese pigeons, golden cocks, and other birds singing. Up a little on the left was a balcony from which one could see in all directions. It was lined with bookshelves, which gave the place a certain studied charm.

"This is our study," the boy told Gengobei, inviting him to sit down. Then he called all the servants. "My guest, the priest, is to be my reading tutor. Please treat him well."

With many things to talk about, they spent the night conversing intimately together. It was so delightful that they felt inspired to make promises of undying friendship. With all their hearts they wished to crowd a thousand nights of love into that one, and next morning the parting was sad.

"Now you are bound for Koya," the boy said in farewell. "On your return do not fail to come and see me again."

When he had quietly stolen away from the house, Gengobei went around to make some inquiries of a man in the village. Among other things he learned that the boy's father was deputy of that region, which made Gengobei still more pleased with his new romance.

The going was slow on his journey toward the capital, so hard was it to pull himself ever farther away from his love, and on the way he thought of nothing but Hachijuro and the new boy. The way to Buddhahood was gone completely from his mind.

At last, reaching the mountain of Kobo, he spent a day in the dormitory for priests, but did not bother to visit even the patriarch's tomb. In no time at all he headed home again, going straight to see the boy as he had promised he would.

The young fellow who greeted him seemed not to have changed a bit since they first met, that day when the boy was birdcatching. Together they went into a small room, where Gengobei began to tell everything that had happened to him. But he was so weary from traveling that he soon dozed off to sleep, unaware that the boy had disappeared.

In the morning the boy's father, surprised to find a stranger there, came in to give him a piece of his mind. Gengobei awoke with a start and hastened to explain everything—how he had come to take up holy orders and what had happened when he came here before. When he had finished, the master gestured with his hands as if at a sudden revelation.

"That is strange indeed! I could not help feeling that he was a singularly beautiful boy, even if he was my own son. But life is never to be counted upon, and twenty days ago the frail creature passed away. Up until the end he kept calling—deliriously, I thought —for a certain priest. Now I see that it was you he meant."

Together they grieved and grieved over the sad loss, and Gengobei wanted to end his life there and then, so little did he value it. But men are not born with a will to die. Having seen two lovers meet death in so short a time, Gengobei found it hard to live on after them. Still, he reckoned it as some extraordinary retribution from the past that he should be required to learn from these two boys what great sadness is. And sad indeed it was.

3. *A lover of men with his hands full of love*

People themselves are the most despicable and heartless of all creatures. If we stop to think and look about us in the world, we find that everyone—ourselves as well as others—talks of giving up his life on the spot when some great misfortune occurs, when a young man dies in the prime of his youthful beauty, or when a wife to whom one has pledged undying love passes away early in life. But even in the midst of tears unseemly desires are ever with us. Our hearts slip off to seek treasure of all kinds or give way to sudden impulses.

Thus it is with the woman whose husband has hardly breathed his last before she is thinking of another man to marry—watching, listening, scheming for one. She may have the dead man's younger brother take his place when he is gone. She may look for a pleasing match among close relatives or, in the dizzy chase, discard completely those with whom she has long been most intimate. She will say one short prayer to Amida —so much for her obligations. She will bring flowers and incense, just so that others may see her do it.

But one can hardly notice when she paints a little powder on her face, impatient to be done with mourning before thirty-five days have passed. Her hair soon regains its luster, glistening with oil, and is all the more attractive because the wanton locks fall free of any hairdress. Then too, her underclothes run riot with color beneath a simple, unadorned garment—so unobtrusive, yet so seductive.

And there is the woman who, feeling the emptiness

of life because of some sad episode, shaves her head in order to spend the rest of her days in a secluded temple, where she will have only the morning dew to offer in memory of her husband, asleep beneath the grass. Among the things she must leave behind is a gown with fawn-spot designs and beautiful embroidery. "I shall not need this anymore. It should be made into a canopy or an altarcloth or a temple pennant." But in her heart the lady is thinking: "Too bad these sleeves are just a little too small. I might still wear them."

Nothing is more dreadful than a woman. No one can keep her from doing what her heart is set upon, and he who tries will be frightened off by a great demonstration of tears. So it is that widows vanish from the earth like ghosts, for none will long be true to a dead man's ghost. And so it is with certain men, except that a man who has killed off three or five wives will not be censured for taking another.

But it was not so with Gengobei. Having seen two lovers die, he was led by true devotion to sequester himself in a grass hut on the mountainside, there to seek earnestly the way to salvation in the afterlife, and to seek naught else, for he had admirably determined to quit the way of the flesh.

At that time in Hama-no-Machi, on the Bay of Satsuma, lived a man from the Ryukyus who had a daughter named Oman. She was fifteen, graced with such beauty that even the moon envied her, and of a gentle, loving disposition. Every man who looked upon her, so ripe for love, wanted her for himself. But in spring of the past year Oman had fallen in love with that flower of manhood, Gengobei. She pined away for him and wrote him many letters, which a messenger delivered in secret. Still there was no answer from Gengobei, who had never in his life given a thought to girls.

It was heartbreaking for Oman. Night and day, day after day, she thought only of him and would consider offers of marriage from no other quarter. She went so far as to feign sudden illness, which puzzled everyone, and she said many wild things to offend people, so that they thought her quite mad. Oman still did not know that Gengobei had become a priest, until one day she heard someone mention the fact. It was a cruel blow, but she tried to console herself, saying that a day would come for her to fulfill her desires, a vain hope indeed, which soon turned to bitter resentment.

"Those black robes of his—how I hate them! I must go to see him just once and let him know how I feel."

With this in mind, Oman bade farewell to her friends as if to leave the world for a nunnery. In secret she clipped her own hair to make it look like a boy's. She had already taken care to get suitable clothing and was able to transform herself completely into a mannish young lover. Then, quietly, stealthily, she set out, bound for the Mountain of Love.

As Oman stepped along she brushed the frost off the bamboo grass, for it was October, the Godless Month,[4] yet here was a girl true to her love. A long way she went, far from the village into a grove of cedars which someone had described to her. At the end of it could be seen the wild crags of a cliff and off to the west a deep cavern, in the depths of which one's mind would get lost thinking about it. Across a stream lay some rotten logs—two, three, four of them, which were barely enough to support her. A treacherous bridge, Oman thought, as she looked down at the rapids below and saw crashing waves which would dash her to pieces. Beyond, on a little piece of flat land, was a lean-to sloping down from the cliff, its eaves all covered with vines from which water dripped, as if it were a "private rain."

On the south side of the hut a window was open.

[4] In October, it was believed, the gods all assembled at the great shrine of Izumo, leaving the rest of the country "godless."

Oman peeped in to find that it was the poorest sort of abode. There was one rickety stove, in which lay a piece of green wood, only half burnt up. There were two big teacups, but no other utensils, not even a dipper or ladle.

"How dismal!" she sighed as she looked around from outside. "Surely the Buddha must be pleased with one who lives in such miserable quarters."

She was disappointed to find the priest gone. "I wonder where to?" she asked, but there was no one there to tell her, nothing at all but the lonely pines, and nothing for her to do but wait, pining among the pines.

Then she tried the door. Luckily it was open. Inside she found a book on his reading table. *The Waiting Bed* it was called, a book which described the origins of manly love.

"Well," she observed, "I see he still has not given up this kind of love."

She thought she would read while waiting for him to return, but soon it grew dark and she could hardly see the words. There was no lamp for her to use and she felt more and more lonely, waiting by herself in the darkness. True love is such that one will endure almost anything for it.

It must have been about midnight when the bonze

Gengobei came home, finding his way by the faint light of a torch. He had almost reached the hut, where Oman waited eagerly for him, when it seemed to her as if two handsome young men came toward him out of the withered underbrush. Each was as beautiful as the other. Either one could have been justly called a "flower of spring" or a "maple leaf in fall." And they seemed to be rivals in love, for one looked resentful and the other deeply hurt. They both made ardent advances toward Gengobei, but he was just one and they were two, and he was helpless to choose between them.

Seeing the agitated, tortured expression on Gengobei's face, Oman could not help feeling a tender sympathy for him. Nevertheless, it was a discouraging sight for her.

"So he has love enough for many men," she said bitterly. "Still, I am committed to this affair and cannot leave it as it stands. I shall simply have to open my heart to him."

Oman went toward him, looking so determined that the two young men took fright and vanished into the night. She, in turn, was startled at their disappearance, and Gengobei at seeing her.

"What sort of young man are you?" he asked.

"As you can see I am one who has taken up the

*He had almost reached the hut, where Oman waited eagerly
for him, when it seemed to her as if two handsome young
men came toward him out of the withered underbrush. Each was as beautiful as the other....*

way of manly love. I have heard so much about you, Sir Priest, that I came all the way to meet you at the risk of my life. But these many loves of yours—I knew nothing of them. I have loved you in vain. It was all a mistake."

In the midst of her wailing Gengobei clapped his hands in delight. "How could I fail to appreciate such love as that!" he exclaimed as his fickle heart went out to her. "Those two lovers you saw are dead—just illusions."

Oman wept and he with her. "Love me in their stead," she begged. "Do not turn me away."

"Love is hard to pass up," he replied coyly, "even for a priest."

Perhaps Buddha would forgive him. After all, Gengobei did not know his lover was a girl.

4. *Variety is the spice of love*

"When I first entered the religious life," Gengobei was saying, "I promised Buddha that I would give up completely the love of women. But I knew it would be very hard to give up the love of young men, and I asked him to be lenient with me in this. Now there is no one who can censure me for it, because I made it all plain to the Buddha from the beginning. Since you loved me enough to come all the way in search of me, you must never forsake me later on."

Gengobei said these things half in jest, but it was doubly a joke for Oman. She pinched her thigh and held her breast to keep from laughing.

"Listen now to what I say," she said in great seriousness. "I was deeply touched by your troubles in the past, and it seems a pity that you should have become a priest. My coming here shows how great was my anguish. I risked my life for your love. From now on you must promise to think no more of taking up with other men. Even if the things I say do not suit you exactly, you must never disobey them. When you have made that solemn pledge, I will give you my all and promise to love you even after death."

It was a foolish thing for Gengobei to do, but he gave his solemn promise. "For a sweetheart like this I would do anything, even leave the priesthood if it came to that."

Panting with desire, he slipped his hand up her sleeve and felt her naked body. It was strange. His lover wore no underwear.[5]

[5] That is, no men's underwear which ties around the waist.

Gengobei's puzzled expression amused Oman, but it was her turn to be puzzled when Gengobei took something from his toilet bag and put it in his mouth to chew on it.

"What are you doing?" she asked.

Without a word he hid whatever it was—perhaps what lovers of men call *nerigi*.[6] This, too, struck Oman as funny and she turned away to lie face downward.

Taking off his clothes, with one foot Gengobei kicked them into a corner and proceeded to the business of love-making, always an absorbing business no matter who you are. He slipped off her sash, which, having been made for a young man, was only of medium width and tied in the rear. Then it occurred to him that his lover might not be accustomed to cool nights in the country, so he threw a large cotton nightrobe over "him."

"Now!" he said, lying down with his head on her arm.

The bonze had hardly settled into bed before he was dizzy with excitement. He ran his hand around her back nervously. "This boy hasn't even a moxa scar yet—hasn't been touched at all."

But when Gengobei began to move his hand slowly down from her hips, it made Oman uneasy. At this

[6] An aphrodisiac made from the hollyhock.

point, she thought, it might be best if she pretended to fall asleep.

Impatient, the bonze began playing with her ear, and she threw one leg over him, revealing some woman's underwear of scarlet crepe.

Gengobei was amazed. He took a careful look at her and realized what a soft face his lover had, just like a woman's. The discovery left him dumbfounded. For a few minutes he could say nothing. Then he tried to get out of bed, but Oman held on to him tightly.

"Before, you promised to do anything I said, no matter what it was. Have you forgotten so soon? I am called Oman of the Ryukyu family. Last year I sent you one love note after another, but you were so unkind as to leave them all unanswered. There was nothing I could do to heal the wound in my heart, nothing but to disguise myself this way and come here to see you. Can you blame me for it?"

When Oman had said this, she brought her lovely young body close to his. In no time at all Gengobei lost himself in a desire for her.

"What difference does it make—the love of men or the love of women?" he cried, overpowered by the bestial passion which rules this fickle world.

Such sudden infatuations are common to us all, not

limited to Gengobei alone. Traps they may be, yet few
can refuse the invitation to fall in. Even one of the
Buddha's feet may have slipped in.

5. *The man who had too much money*

It takes only a year to grow a head of hair. When
he had cast off his holy robes, the young bonze looked
like the old Gengobei, and he started calling himself
by that name again.

In the mountains, where there are no calendars,
people tell the seasons by the blooming and falling of
the plum blossoms. It was January when Gengobei
gave up monastic abstinence for a life of idle pleasure.
In early February he went to see an old friend
who lived outside Kagoshima and rented from him
a little thatched cottage where he could live in
seclusion with Oman. But as they had no means of
livelihood, Gengobei went to visit the home of his
parents, only to find that it had been sold into other
hands. What once had been a respectable money-
changer's office no longer knew the ring of gold and
silver on metal scales. Near the entrance was now hung

a sign reading "Bean-curd," the sight of which made Gengobei sick at heart.

He asked a stranger: "What has happened to the man Gengoemon who used to live around here?"

"I have heard," the stranger told him, "that he was once a good and prosperous man. He had a son called Gengobei, the handsomest young man of this province, but also a slave to love. In eight years time Gengobei wasted over eight thousand pounds of silver on his pleasures, and the loss unfortunately meant ruination for the old man, which just goes to show how things can turn out. Later on, they say, Gengobei gave up the world of pleasure for the life of a monk, all because of some love affair. Can you imagine being as thoughtless as that? Whenever people speak of him, they say: 'I'd just like to meet that rascal once, face to face!'"

"That face is right here," Gengobei thought to himself, and out of shame he pulled his straw hat far down over his head.

At last he returned to his lodging place, where there was no lamp to see by at night and no firewood for chilly mornings. What was even more depressing, love and love-making did not thrive on hard times. The lovers slept side-by-side on the same pillow, but had nothing to say to each other in the way of bedtime talk.

Then morning came and it was March third, the

day of the Doll's Festival. Little boys ran about with presents of bean cakes for their relatives. Outside there were cockfights and various other amusements. But still it was a dreary day inside for the lovers. They had not even a sardine to put upon the tray set before the altar. They broke off a sprig of peach blossom and, since there was no saké, set the blossoms in their empty saké jar. That was all. When day faded into night, the fourth followed in dismal succession.

Once, as they were thinking of a way to earn a living, it occurred to them to put on plays such as they had once seen in the capital. In no time at all Gengobei made up his face with a false mustache so that he looked the part of the gallant Slave to Love.[7] Indeed he seemed the living image of the actor Arashi Sanemon,[8] except that his carriage on the stage was poor because his hips swayed like an amateur's.

"Yakkono, yakkono,"[9] he sang. And then:

> *Gengobei, where did you go?*
> *To the hills of Satsuma,*
> *With a scabbard worth three cents,*
> *And a sword-knot only two,*
> *And a sword inside of cypress wood.*

[7] Gengobei himself, as portrayed in the theatre in Saikaku's time.
[8] Famous actor of Saikaku's time who played the role of Gengobei.
[9] Rhythmic chant, introducing a popular song about Gengobei.

While he sang thus in a loud voice to amuse the children of one village after another, Oman dressed herself up in faded garments to perform *kyogen*[10] and other dramatic acts. Together they lived along in a world where tears were as plentiful as dew. It was not easy living on love. They had to lose all sense of pride and wore themselves thinner each day until their old beauty was lost too. Still, in this cruel world, there was no one who felt any pity for them. They were as helpless against fate as the purple blossoms of the wisteria, doomed to fade and die. They cursed their friends, pitied themselves. At last it seemed as if the end had come.

Then it so happened that Oman's parents came along, anxiously searching for their daughter. When they found her it was an occasion for great rejoicing. They decided that, since Gengobei was the man of Oman's heart, the two should be united in wedlock and given the family home and fortune. A whole retinue of servants came to escort them home, where their return brought joy to all.

To Gengobei were turned over all the keys to the family possessions, three hundred and eighty-three of them. A date was set for the wedding and the storage cellar was opened up. In it were great trays

[10] *Kyogen*—in this case an early form of Kabuki.

While he sang thus in a loud voice ... Oman dressed herself up in faded garments to perform ... dramatic acts. Together they lived along in a world where tears were as plentiful as dew. It was not easy living on love....

of money, six hundred and fifty of them, each marked "82 pounds of silver." All the coins were covered with mould and seemed to have beeen hidden away for so long that one could almost hear them groaning to be let out of confinement.

In the northeast corner of the cellar stood seven large jars, full of newly-minted coins that spilled out through the cover and lay about like sand littering the floor. Outside in a separate storehouse there was a mountain of fine clothes which had originally come from China, and a piece of aloewood as large as the beam on which a cauldron is hung over a fire. There were one thousand two hundred and thirty-five flawless coral beads, weighing from one and a half to one hundred and thirty *momme* each; sharkskin for sword handles; celadon porcelain in unlimited quantities; fine teacups from the Asuka River region, piled about carelessly because it made no difference how many got broken; some salted Mermaids;[11] a small bucket made of agate; a rice pounder from the Taoist paradise of Han-tan in China; a kitchen-knife box from Old Urashima;[12] a scarf from Benzaiten, Goddess of Beauty; a razor made for the long-headed Fukurokuju, God of Luck; the spear of Tamon, Guardian of Heaven; a winnow from

[11] A kind of salamander.
[12] The submarine palace of the goddess Otohime.

*To Gengobei were turned over all the keys to the family
possessions ... great trays of money ... a mountain of fine
clothes ... celadon porcelain ... salted Mermaids
... all the treasures of the world....*

the God of Plenty large enough to winnow five thousand bushels of rice; and so many other things that one could not remember them all. Indeed, all the treasures of the world were there.

Gengobei was so happy that he wept.

"I could buy up all the beauties of Edo, Kyoto, and Osaka.[13] I could finance all the theatres.[14] And still it would take more than my lifetime to spend this whole fortune. No matter how hard I tried, I could not think of a way to use the money up. What in the world will I do with it?"

[13] The top-ranking female prostitutes (*tayu*), whose debts he would have to pay off to make them his own.

[14] With their male actor-prostitutes.

Saikaku's "Five Women"

Richard Lane
Columbia University

It is only in the past sixty years that the greatness of the Japanese novelist Ihara Saikaku (1642–1693) has come generally to be recognized in his own country. Not, of course, that he was neglected in his own day; his works were best sellers, and other novelists copied and plagiarized him assiduously. But the novelist had no status, no *raison d'être,* in a feudal society. It remained for the opening of Japan in the mid-nineteenth century—with the subsequent realization of the importance of the novelist in Europe, and a familiarity with the new literary currents of naturalism and realism—to make Japanese intellectuals seek in their own past a spirit they could call teacher and preceptor. Thus the Saikaku revival came largely at the hands of the novelists, among them the greatest figures of the Meiji Enlightenment—Kōda Rohan, Ozaki Kōyō, Mori Ōgai, and Higuchi Ichiyō.

Although *Five Women Who Loved Love*[1] has always been one of the most popular of Saikaku's works of fiction, its significance in Japanese cultural history is not readily apparent to the modern reader. We can only with effort project ourselves into a feudal and Procrustean age in which no men were created equal, each having his own strictly hierarchical place in society. Only when, in Saikaku's novels, an anti-conventional love affair is punished by the death penalty, are we forcibly reminded of the inclement age in which he wrote. And only after examining the conventionalized writings of Saikaku's predecessors and contemporaries do we realize what a daring innovator for egalitarianism he was.

Saikaku has thus a special significance for Americans: some two and a half centuries ago he planted the seeds of that democracy which found opportunity for renewed growth under our own recent Occupation. Saikaku wrote:[2] "Even a court nobleman, deprived of his ceremonial robes, becomes but a plaster-peddler possessed of a rather pale skin. Man is in general only what his profession makes him." Here he was expressing a way of thought rare in pre-modern Japanese literature—an idea which had hardly as yet gained any wide currency in Europe.

Without some knowledge of Saikaku's times, his full significance cannot be apprehended. Thus, in addition to discussing the literary elements of *Five Women Who Loved Love,* we shall have occasion subsequently to examine in some detail the legal and social conditions that form the background of his stories.

[1] *Kōshoku gonin onna.* The title might also be rendered *Love and Five Women,* or *Five Women Who Gave Themselves to Love.*
[2] *A Mirror of the Beauties (Shoen ōkagami),* 1684.

*   *   *

Saikaku was forty-four years old when he wrote *Five Women Who Loved Love*. He had already, some four years earlier, given up a successful career as poet and critic in order to devote himself to the as yet unrecognized profession of novel writing. From the brilliant but erratic performance in his first novel, *The Love Rogue (Kōshoku ichidai otoko)* of 1682, Saikaku had progressed through a series of novels and stories which portrayed in detail the varied facets of the life and loves of his times—the adventures of gallants and rakes, of courtesans and harlots, of samurai and plebeian pederasts. Now, with the year 1686, he turned from the world of socially and legally sanctioned love and sensuality and set his scene amidst the common men and women of the towns, depicting freedom of love in an age when this was the most dangerous of all games.

Only a year earlier Saikaku had published his first novel based upon the life of an actual person—*The Life and Death of Wankyū (Wankyū isse no monogatari)*. Now he took for his protagonists five contemporary heroines—from their tragic lives weaving the tales published together as *Five Women Who Loved Love*. The five novelettes are analyzed below.[3]

Book One: Onatsu and Seijūrō

As with each of the five stories in *Five Women Who Loved Love*, this novelette is divided into five chapters. In the first

[3] The following material is derived in part from my *Saikaku: Novelist of the Japanese Renaissance*, and several of my original translated excerpts from Saikaku have been retained. Since no translation can

is introduced the hero Seijūrō, handsome son of a wealthy townsman, an experienced gallant, beloved of all the courtesans. To us, profligacy may not seem a very suitable qualification for a romantic hero; but in a society where marriages were arranged by one's parents, where the niceties of courtship were hardly known, and where love affairs with ordinary townswomen were highly perilous, the gay quarters were the only training ground for a connoisseur of love. Saikaku's purpose in this opening chapter is simply to show the hero's qualifications for the more serious love affair that is to follow in the succeeding chapters. Seijūrō is thus introduced as an idealized gallant, reminiscent of the famous hero of Saikaku's first novel, *The Love Rogue.*

Having introduced his hero, and furthermore, in the affair with Minagawa, shown his capacity for serious love, Saikaku in his second chapter enters into the main story, for which his hero has been prepared by disownment for his earlier follies. Here Seijūrō displays his basic qualities as a member of the bourgeoisie, and proves a dependable and energetic worker. This situation is upset by the master's younger sister Onatsu, who, though already fifteen,[4] and romantically inclined, has as yet refused all offers of marriage. And what first turns her heart toward Seijūrō is not his handsomeness, but rather the

recreate this author's remarkable style, these excerpts by a different hand may be of interest in indicating other possible renderings of the text. For information on the best texts and most recent studies of *Five Women Who Loved Love*, the reader is referred to my "Postwar Japanese Studies of the Novelist Saikaku," in the *Harvard Journal of Asiatic Studies* for 1955. For an earlier translation from the work and a general discussion of Saikaku, see my "Ihara Saikaku: Realistic Novelist of the Tokugawa Period," in the *Journal of Oriental Literature* for 1948.

[4]Sixteen by Japanese count; this was the normal age for marriage.

thought of the remarkable qualifications he must possess, to have been so sincerely loved by so many courtesans! Seijūrō is at first reluctant to forego his peace of mind, but once having returned the girl's affection, it is he who plans the details of the picnic in the third chapter, in order that they may be alone together. Here, as in one such passage in each of the other four stories of the book, the scene of the lover's first bliss is described suggestively, though with considerable restraint.[5]

In the fourth chapter the lovers elope, for Seijūrō's lowly position as an employee renders hope of an approved marriage impossible. The coincidental mislaying of seven hundred *ryō* in gold seems a rather artificial device to increase our sympathies for the lovers, but this was probably one of the conventions of the story as it appeared in the popular theatre of the time. Again, one might even suggest that this was but a ruse on the author's part to avoid direct criticism of the Tokugawa laws against love between unequals, which was, after all, the only actual "crime" involved. Further, it was very common in this period for eloping couples to steal and take such funds with them; and as we shall see, Saikaku's story is based upon an actual event. At any rate, Seijūrō's fate is sealed on all three counts of seduction, kidnaping, and theft, and he is beheaded. The final chapter turns back to Onatsu, who is left behind to suffer madness and final retirement from the world of men.

Sources and background. The actual events of this story occurred in Himeji about the years 1659–60. There is no

[5] The description of the lovers is straightforward enough, but the inclusion of the woodcutter in this scene is clearly a lubricious intrusion, derived from one of the more common conventions of Japanese pornographic art—that of depicting a masturbating spectator on the side lines of an erotic scene.

reliable contemporary account of the event, Saikaku's story being
the oldest now extant. We do possess, however, a rare ballad
of the *utazaimon* genre entitled *Onatsu and Seijūrō,* part of a
series on the subject of the "Five Women Who Loved Love"
and dating probably from the 1690's. The ballad is too long to
quote in full, but may be summarized as follows, for comparison
with Saikaku's version:

Onatsu and the employee Seijūrō were deeply in love, but
Onatsu's father, not knowing of their affair, had already
arranged for her marriage. Kanshichi, another employee of
the House of Tajima, pilfered Onatsu's marriage trousseau and
dowry money and informed his master that Seijūrō had committed the theft in order to obstruct the forthcoming marriage.
The father became terribly angry, for he had only with great
difficulty succeeded in arranging an advantageous marriage for
his daughter, who had been born of a courtesan and was thus
not acceptable in a high-class family. The father expelled Seijūrō at once. Seijūrō plotted that very night to stab the false
accuser Kanshichi in his bed, but by mistake he killed another
employee. For this he was taken prisoner and soon after
executed.

Despite the fact that part of their purpose lay in the recita-
tion of newsworthy happenings, the *utazaimon* ballads as a
genre were quite free in their treatment of actual events and
were characterized particularly by the intensification of dramatic
elements. Thus such details as Onatsu's parentage—daughter of
a courtesan of Murotsu[6]—seem added for greater dramatic in-

[6] The seaport where, according to Saikaku's version, young Seijūrō
sowed his wild oats. Situated about 15 miles west of Himeji, it was
a major stopover point for the daimyō of West Japan on their way to
Edo and was famous for its gay quarter.

tensity, as does likewise the introduction of the villain Kanshichi, the mistaken stabbing (a convention of such tales), and
possibly even the proposed marriage itself, which produced a
dramatic crisis for the lovers.

But let us examine another version of the story, that appearing in Nishizawa Ippū's novel of 1718, *Three Revenges for
Adultery (Midare-hagi sambon yari)*:

Seijūrō, an employee of the House of Tajima, was carrying
on a secret affair with his master's daughter Onatsu. The two
eloped to Osaka, but were captured and taken back to Himeji.
Seijūrō was beheaded. After her parents died, having no near
relatives or friends, Onatsu removed to Katakami in the province of Bizen, where she opened a little teashop for travelers
and lived to an old age.

Ippū's version seems nearer to the true events. The story
occurs in his novel as an incidental anecdote concerning the
village of Katakami and there is no attempt at dramatization.
It will be seen that his version is basically the same as that used
by Saikaku, who, however, inserts an introductory chapter on
Seijūrō's background and then at the end adds, perhaps from
his own imagination, the story of Onatsu's madness and becoming a nun.

To the above literary sources must be added a recently discovered semi-historical one, which, though dating from a century
after the actual event, may well be the most accurate of all.
This account appears in the manuscript *Shoki shishūki* of 1760
and will be translated in full, retaining the elliptical style of
the original:

Memorandum on the Affair of Onatsu and Seijūrō
The second house from the corner at the Fuda Crossroads,

Main Street, Himeji, was formerly that of Kuzaemon of the House of Tajima; at present the house is occupied by the clan official Omoteya Shirobei. Behind it there is an old well used for drainage, i.e., the well in use there during the period under consideration.

The clerk Seijūrō was a native of Murotsu. Following his dismissal from employment he rented a house on Nishi-kon Street. Saying that it was for the purpose of breaking in, he had a sword made. Every evening a man named Kakoya Shōzaemon from Sakata Street tried to dissuade him.

On a certain day in the Sixth Month of 1659, the Year of the Wild Boar, Seijūrō broke in. As the father Kuzaemon was escaping from the house, he tripped over a barley-drying mat at the opposite north side of the street and fell down. Thereupon Seijūrō slashed him from behind, wounding him on the shoulder. From the neighborhood, people gathered but were unable to capture Seijūrō. The clan police were called, and Seijūrō was put in jail. Afterwards, at the foot of Sembakawa Road, at the eastern edge of the Ichimai Bridge, he was beheaded.

His grave is behind the Kyūshō Hermitage (in front of the Keiun Temple), an appendage of the Nozato Keiun Temple, and is marked by a pine tree, still standing. It is said that Onatsu later went to Shōdo Island to be married; this is according to Aboshiya Dōsei.

Seijūrō had been taken in and concealed for a time in the Kyūshō Hermitage. For this, the front gate was closed by official order.

The above affair of Onatsu and Seijūrō was made into Jōruri and Kabuki plays and became famous.

The Emperor Gosai has a verse:

> *Seijūrō—*
> *Has not Onatsu [summer] come,*
> *The weeping cuckoo-bird?*
> *The straw hat so resembles his:*
> *O Moon of Ariake.*

Although a late source, in its relative simplicity this account may well represent the true story. The details of Seijūrō's dismissal are not given, but presumably the occasion was the discovery of his affair with Onatsu (who in this account also is the *daughter* of Kuzaemon). For revenge, Seijūrō broke into the House of Tajima, wounded his former master, and for this was subsequently executed.

It will be seen that any attempt to reconcile these varied sources must remain tentative and unresolved. Although the early Kabuki versions of the tale have been lost, they may well have exerted a strong influence upon Saikaku's treatment of the story, particularly in simplifying the lover's crime to love alone, whereas in the actual event an attempt at murder was also involved.

In this connection it is interesting to note that Chikamatsu, in his dramatic version of the story, produced in 1709 under the title *A Prayer-Song to Buddha on the Fiftieth Anniversary (Gojūnenki uta-nembutsu),* follows the aforementioned *utazaimon* ballad rather closely. In this he was doubtless adhering to the theatrical tradition that had early developed around the story of the two lovers.[7]

---

[7] Whatever ballads or dramas preceded the *utazaimon* have been lost. We have, however, an interesting record that they did exist, and within a few years after the actual events. Thus in the recently discovered *Diary of Matsudaira, Lord of Yamato,* written by a daimyō devotee of

It should not be concluded, however, that the variations between Saikaku's version on the one hand and that of the *uta-zaimon* and Chikamatsu on the other are entirely a matter of the differing requirements of the novel and the drama. Rather is this due to a basically different attitude toward life.

Throughout *Five Women Who Loved Love* the actual crimes of Saikaku's lovers are those of love alone. That Saikaku should have been the first Japanese writer to treat the subject in such detail will indicate his sympathies; at the same time, he does not evade the direct consequences. With Chikamatsu's hero, the mistaken stabbing doubtless increases our sympathy for the man, but it also enables the dramatist to evade punishing his creature for his actual crime—forbidden love. Saikaku is not able openly to criticize the laws of his country, yet he lets his readers see clearly that—whatever the immediate causes of execution—his protagonist's crimes are primarily those of passion alone.

Chikamatsu's characters are guilty primarily of unfiliality and disloyalty—the daughter to her father (who had gone to such trouble to arrange a good marriage) and Seijūrō to his master. But Saikaku's protagonists are the more tragic: their crimes are human, natural, and uncontrived; they are victims not of Fate nor of the wrath of the gods, but of feudal law.

the popular theatre, we find the following notation for the Fourth Month of 1664: "The most popular song these days in Edo is the 'Seijūrō Ballad.' It has come into popularity since the time it was made into a play at the [Nakamura] Kanzaburō Theatre...." From this it is clear that the event, occurring in a distant western province, was already well known in the Edo Kabuki within three or four years after it took place. Even without this evidence, however, the great popularity which followed Saikaku's revival of the story would indicate that it had been widely known in its own day and never quite forgotten during the subsequent two decades.

Finally, let us examine something of this law that governed seventeenth-century Japanese society:[8]

Item One. Illicit intercourse. Persons such as those who have engaged in illicit intercourse with their master's daughter, or who have attempted such: Death. *At the master's request this may be reduced to banishment to a distant island, or may be pardoned.*[9]

Item Two. Abduction.[10] *In accordance with previous examples: Those who abduct persons:* Death.

Item Three. Theft. [No specific edict is known for the seventeenth century; the following edict, approved in 1720 and again in 1741, doubtless applied equally to the earlier period, when in fact, most punishments were more strict.] *Those who take things given in their charge and flee with them: When money, more than ten ryō,*[11] *and when goods, of a value exceeding ten ryō:* Death.

It must be added that, although not always specifically so stated, the punishment depended to a considerable degree upon the relationship of the offender to the offended. Illicit intercourse as such was not necessarily punished if both parties were of equal rank and no criminal offence was involved.

The Confucian ideals of piety and loyalty to one's master or teacher played, of course, an important role in the make-up of

[8] The codes, together with the other legal data included in the present study, are derived primarily from the following Edo-period sources: *Genroku gohōshiki, Osadamegaki hyakkajō, Oshioki reiruishū Kajō ruiten, Genroku keiten,* and *Oshioki saikyochō.*

[9] A master's younger sister, though not mentioned specifically, would presumably be treated similarly to his daughter.

[10] *Kadowakashi.* Usually implying slaving, abduction, or kidnaping, this term included also the crime of "causing a girl to elope with one."

[11] Ten *ryō* in gold was worth about three hundred dollars.

Tokugawa law. But perhaps more basic was the fact that *shame* (on the part of the injured) was the moralizing force in Tokugawa society, where *guilt* (on the part of the offender) would be in ours. A menial's crime was thus the greater, for he made his master suffer a terrible loss of face—which might even cause the latter's social or financial ruin. Thus, with the wife of an employer or teacher, or with his daughter, the punishment for illicit intercourse was often death. With the younger married sister of one's wife, with one's mother-in-law, or with another man's wife (if an equal), however, the punishment was usually only banishment. Such laws were not consistent, however, and there were frequent changes, particularly in the eighteenth century. Thus, for example, an edict of 1741 states: "A man who seduces his master's daughter is to be sentenced to medium deportation. The daughter, however, is to be handcuffed and turned over to her parents."

Psychologically, the most important factor to remember is that the accused, if wanting in influence, had no legal means of redress or appeal.

Book Two: Osen the Cooper's Wife

The first notable element in this tale is the low social rank of the protagonists. Osen is an unlettered peasant girl, come to Osaka to work as a servant in order to help her impoverished family. The cooper is an artisan; and the old woman who effects their meeting, a former abortionist now making her living by grinding flour. This totally plebeian atmosphere marks a new element in Japanese literature.

Next should be noted the readiness with which Osen, who has had no relations with men before, accepts the cooper's suit. True, the cooper's cause is put forward very skillfully by the old woman, and Osen may be supposed just to be reaching the age for romantic thoughts. But at the same time her enthusiastic acceptance, before she has even seen the man, indicates in her an uncommon susceptibility to the feminine weakness for being loved. This trait, in a way, prepares the reader for that act of willful passion that is to end the heroine's life.[12]

Saikaku's emphasis upon the events leading up to Osen's marriage, rather than upon the later tragedy itself, may best be understood when we recollect that he was writing of an actual event that had occurred but a year earlier. He purposely, therefore, prolonged the preliminary story of the romance of Osen and the cooper, bringing in the incident of the pilgrimage to Ise and the obstructive character Kyūshichi, and effecting the marriage only toward the end of the last chapter but one. The very fact that the organization of the volume required five chapters for each novelette perhaps also influenced his treatment of the plot.

Finally, at the end of the fourth chapter Saikaku gives a general picture of the current low state of wifely morality, by way of preparing the reader for the events of the final chapter. This moralizing must be taken as representing one facet of Saikaku's own views, for though he was radical for his times in advocating freedom in the choice of a mate, irrespective of

[12]Compare La Rochefoucauld's dictum of about the same period (*Maximes*, 1665–78): "Women often think themselves to be in love when they are not. Their natural passion for being beloved, their unwillingness to give a denial, the excitement of mind produced by an affair of gallantry, all these make them imagine they are in love, when in fact they are only acting the coquette."

social rank, this did not extend to condoning adultery, or even remarriage on the part of a widow. It is important to stress the fact that although Saikaku sympathized even with adulteresses, he could not condone the morality of their act.

The climax of the story is handled only briefly, and it is not the attempt at adultery which interests Saikaku so much as the psychological motivation of Osen, a happily married mother. There is no indication that she preferred the elderly Chōzaemon to her own husband; what moved her was primarily indignation at Chōzaemon's wife. Her revenge took the only form that occurred to her—actually carrying out the act of which she had been unjustly accused.

The ability to create an infatuation out of her own imagination had been but an amusing characteristic of Osen's when first revealed earlier in the story; now it was to prove her destruction.

Sources and background. Regarding the sources of this story, we possess no historical data at all. The date given for the final incident in Saikaku's story is the First Month of 1685, the festival evening of the twenty-second day—less than a year before the novel was written. We have nothing to confirm or deny this date. The only other contemporary version of the story is the *utazaimon* ballad *Taruya Osen* (Osen the Cooper's Wife), evidently current at the time Saikaku's novel was written, though the oldest extant version dates from a decade later. As we have noted in discussing the sources of the Onatsu-Seijūrō story, the *utazaimon* ballads tended to melodramatize the actual events and often introduced fictional incidents to that end. The *Taruya Osen* ballad tells this story:

The Osaka cooper Chūbyōe and his wife Osen were a loving

couple, with a son of four named Matsu-no-suke. One evening, while the cooper was out at a temple service, the neighborhood malt merchant Chōemon, who was in love with Osen, came visiting and attempted to force his attentions upon her. Osen refused him, whereupon he took hold of her son, who was sleeping nearby, and threatened to kill the boy with a dagger. Out of love for her child Osen conceded to Chōemon's desire. Just at that moment her husband returned home. Osen killed herself on the spot, knowing excuses to be of no avail. She was but twenty-two when she died.

In the absence of historical data it is not possible to state categorically which version is nearer to the events; yet the *utazaimon* scene of the threatened child is an obviously theatrical one and quite probably an invention. Certainly the incident of the dropped tray and Osen's consequent impulsive actions—the weakest points in Saikaku's story—would not have been sufficiently melodramatic for a sentimental popular ballad. Thus it may well be that the dramatic deficiencies of Saikaku's final chapter are due primarily to an overadherence to the actual facts of the story. At the same time it is noteworthy that the *utazaimon*—which doubtless represents the popular concept of the event—concentrates entirely upon the immediate scene of the adultery. The first four chapters of Saikaku's novel would thus seem his own invention (though perhaps based upon some other contemporary event)—probably added from a feeling that the adultery scene alone did not offer sufficient material for a novelette of this length.

Regarding the legal aspects of Saikaku's story and of the events behind it, the laws are most clear in cases concerning adultery with the wife of one's master:

Persons such as those who commit adultery with their master's wife, or with their teacher's wife: Death for both the man and the woman.

Persons such as those who propose adultery, or those who send love letters to their master's wife: Death, banishment, or pardon.[13]

Persons accessory to adultery with a master's wife: Death.[14]

Although not considered so great a crime, adultery with the wife of an equal was technically punishable likewise, though such cases were rare, and the severity of the punishment in this case must certainly have startled the bourgeois society of the day. Chōzaemon's crime was doubtless intensified by the fact of Osen's immediate suicide—just as, in cases of double suicide, when the lover failed to die he was often executed anyway.

Several edicts explicitly state, moreover, that a husband who finds his wife in the act of adultery may legally execute both her and the lover on the spot. Osen's immediate suicide thus had its basis not only in shame at discovery, but also in a clear awareness of her probable fate. Whether she thought of the consequences before that actual moment is difficult to say.

BOOK THREE: OSAN AND MOEMON

Of the five stories which comprise *Five Women Who Loved Love* the third is the most skillfully organized. The opening

[13] "Pardon" often indicated that the offender could go without punishment if the plaintiff so requested. In other cases, offenders could sometimes be pardoned if they had relatives willing to guarantee their future conduct.

[14] This last instance refers to servants who conveyed love letters or arranged the meeting of such lovers.

chapter, in which the rakes of Kyoto (among them Osan's future husband) survey the different women passing by, is an excellent introduction to the heroine Osan, delineating not only her beauty, but also evoking the sensuous atmosphere that is to suffuse the whole story.[15] The introduction brings in no conflicting elements and leads naturally into the revelation of who this girl is and where her beauty is to lead her.[16]

Although the events surrounding Osan's marriage to the almanac maker are dealt with only briefly, the marriage has something in common with that of Osen, namely, that the proposal came from the man's side and was accepted without the girl's knowing her future husband. The character, education, and social status of the two girls are of course quite different. But they do have in common this element of passive acceptance of love, and doubtless it is one of the factors underlying their subsequent rash behavior.

Not unlike the mortification Osen feels at the unjust accusations of Chōzaemon's wife is the indignation felt by Osan when she reads Moemon's churlish reply to the letter she has written him on Rin's behalf:

"Why, how abominable he is! There's certainly no dearth of men in this world! Rin's as pretty as they come and should

[15] The frame of this chapter is doubtless derived from the "Critique of Women" scene in Book II of *The Tale of Genji*.

[16] The technique of describing the passing crowd as a method of creating the atmosphere of a scene was apparently an innovation of Saikaku's. It first occurs two years earlier in his *Mirror of the Beauties* (Book V, 5), wherein a group of young men examine critically the fair women passing by on their way to the Shitennō Temple in Osaka. (There, however, it is only a sketch, the young men concluding that the only real beauties are the courtesans.) It is quite possible that Saikaku derived this technique from the genre scrolls and prints of the *ukiyo-e* school, of which he was himself a notable exponent.

*hardly have trouble finding a lover the equal of this fellow
Moemon anytime."*

*And so she determined to write a movingly tearful appeal
to him, this time breaking down all his reserve and making
him her fool....*

Thus it is through pride and loss of face (whether felt per-
sonally, or as an insult to one's sex) that both women seal their
fate.

Osan's seduction represents one of the most interesting facets
of Saikaku's studies in female psychology. Let us analyze the
scene:

Osan, an oversexed young wife; her doting husband away in
the distant city of Edo. An exciting affair afoot: tonight the
handsome clerk Moemon is (though somewhat begrudgingly)
to seduce the maid Rin. By Osan's scheme, however, he is to
be tricked and made fun of, finding, instead, his mistress in
the bed!

Here is all the "excitement of an affair of gallantry" that La
Rochefoucauld knew so well. Such pranks, clearly a sexual
outlet, could hardly fail to arouse Osan's sexual curiosity and
required very little to divert them toward the real act.

And this leads us to inquire: *Was Osan really asleep?* On
the surface, Saikaku's text would seem to indicate that she
was. Yet to Saikaku's readers the situation of a beautiful and
proud young wife left alone in the midst of temptation connoted
certain logical conclusions—which Boccaccio's readers would
have understood well enough, though today we prefer to
consider such as "exceptions." By the same token, to us the
word "widow" brings to mind a kindly-faced lady struggling
to support starving infants. In Saikaku's time there was already

a proverb: "Show me a widow not engulfed in the mists of passion!" In effect, "widow" connoted "nymphomaniac."[17]

Having said this much, the final decision regarding Osan's behavior may be left to the reader. In the end, this may depend more upon experience and philosophy of life than upon a reanalysis of Saikaku's text. Whichever the case, Osan's reaction is immediate: "There can be no hope of keeping this matter secret. The best that can be done now is to abandon my life to the affair, embrace the name of scandal for what time remains, and in the end find Moemon my companion on the road to hell."

Raised with care in a wealthy bourgeois family and wed at the age of thirteen or fourteen to a middle-aged stranger, Osan is yet possessed of a strong will of her own. Now, at the age of sixteen she finds her first opportunity—albeit perhaps a fortuitous one—to follow a love of her own accord. With both Osan and Osen, it is this need for self-assertion that proves their undoing. And therein doubtless lies the true meaning of the *kōshoku* ("in love with love") of Saikaku's title.

Once having made her decision and expecting death at any minute, Osan for the first time finds what love is really like, and is no longer so ready to quit life. Thus, when the lovers journey to Lake Biwa, in the back of their minds hovers the shadow of death. Yet when Osan broaches the subject, she is lacking in resolution; and when Moemon suggests they run away instead, Osan is delighted and shows him the five hundred

[17] On the subject of passionate widows, see my translation of Saikaku's "The Umbrella Oracle," in *Anthology of Japanese Literature* (New York, 1955; edited by Donald Keene); also, "The Widow and the Fortunate Gallant," included in my "Saikaku and Boccaccio: The *Novella* in Japan and Italy," to appear shortly in the *Journal of World History*.

ryō in gold which she had brought along with that very course in mind.[18]

In the fourth chapter the principal subject is the depiction of the degree to which this passion for love has taken hold of Osan's heart. Thus as the lovers struggle through the unknown wilds in their flight, when Osan drops from exhaustion it is the pleading words of Moemon that revive her.

Again later, warned in a dream (or in her own conscience) of the consequences of her folly, Osan hears herself answering the god: "Please do not concern yourself with what becomes of us; for this is our delight: a love, however criminal, for which we'd pay our very lives...."

That end is not far distant; but first Saikaku shows something more of the character of Moemon, drawn into this love despite himself and now longing to see the capital again.

It is soon after that the two are discovered. Their end is depicted simply, with compassion: "It was the twenty-second day of the Ninth Month, their final moments like a swiftly evanescent dream at dawn; yet never ignoble nor soon forgotten by the world. Even now her form, sheathed in the pale-blue gown she wore that day, lingers in the inner eye together with her name of love."

Sources and background. The affair of Osan and Moemon occurred only two or three years prior to Saikaku's novel, the date of execution being given variously as 1683 or 1684. The

[18] The *michiyuki* sequence in this chapter, which describes the lovers' journey in terms of the passing scenes they view, is an intrusion from the Jōruri drama. Though an excellent piece of writing in itself, for the modern reader it may tend to detract from the realism of the story. The concept of "realism" was, however, only now being developed by Saikaku, and such poetic elements were rather expected by his readers.

Nishijin tengu hikki cites the latter date, recording that Osan was of a poor family in Tamba Province and was eighteen at the time of her marriage. At the execution grounds, Dōjō, the head priest of the Kinzan Tennō Temple, attempted to intercede for the lovers, but the calendar maker's strong opposition rendered this impossible.[19]

Another semi-historical source gives the date as the Ninth Month of 1683, the calendar maker's name as Ishun, the lover's name as Mohei, and the servant girl's name as Tama.[20] The lovers are said to have fled with the maidservant to Tamba, where they were captured, brought back to the capital, led around the streets as a warning to others, and then executed. As for the degree of punishment, Osan and Mohei were crucified, whereas Tama was decapitated and her head exposed to view. Mohei's three brothers, who had given the criminals shelter, were banished. On account of the scandal, the calendar maker was forced to abandon his profession.

The *utazaimon* ballad version is in this case less melodramatic than usual: When the calendar maker Ishun went on a journey to Edo, Mohei, with the servant Tama as go-between, became intimate with his wife Osan. When Osan became noticeably pregnant, the lovers fled to Tamba; but they were soon discovered, brought back to Kyoto, and executed.

[19] The official calendar maker held a position of some importance. Though a townsman, he was accorded the privilege of employing a surname and received a yearly stipend from the shōgun.

[20] Saikaku calls the girl Rin throughout the second chapter of the novelette. Then, in the execution scene, he employs the name Tama. The latter was apparently the real name of the girl, which he let slip in inadvertently. (The change from Mohei to Moemon is similar to that from Chōemon to Chōzaemon in the Osen story.) Note that Chika-matsu in his famous dramatic version of the story, noted later, employs the actual names as they are given in the above source.

Despite certain differences of detail in these versions, it seems clear that most of the incidents of Saikaku's novel are entirely imaginative, following only the general outline of the actual events. It is probably for this reason that he is more successful here in developing a unified plot than in some of the other stories of the collection. As a heroine, Osan is perhaps the most remarkable of his creations.

This story, treated also by Chikamatsu in his Jōruri drama *Daikyōji mukashi-goyomi*[21] of 1715, has long been a favorite among students wishing to compare the differing characteristics of these two great writers. Since Chikamatsu's work is available in English, we need not elaborate the point here and will simply outline his version briefly:

The clerk Mohei, grateful for assistance rendered him by the maidservant Tama, visits her bedroom. Osan, to rebuke her lustful husband Ishun (who is trying to force his attentions on the maid Tama) is waiting in Tama's bed for her husband, but unwittingly receives Mohei. Knowing concealment of their mistake to be impossible, the two flee together. After various complications they are captured, but when about to be executed are saved by an influential priest.

Chikamatsu's play is an excellent work of the Jōruri genre and should be judged with the particular requirements of the puppet theatre in mind. It is clear, however, that Chikamatsu —though considerably influenced by Saikaku's version of the story—has frequently substituted theatrical artificiality for realistic motivation. In Saikaku's novelette the initial mistake, whether intentional or not, has definite implications and roots

[21] There is a free translation in A. Miyamori's *Masterpieces of Chikamatsu* (London, 1926) under the title "The Almanac of Love."

in the mind of Osan; it is not just a comedy of errors. Chikamatsu's final *deus ex machina* twist may be highly gratifying to
the anxious audience of the puppet drama; but to the realistic
Saikaku the characters would lose significance if they missed
the fate they had so long dreaded.

The legal implications of the affair involve the edicts already
quoted concerning Osen. Here, however, the crime is greater
as being perpetrated by a servant upon his master's wife, and
this doubtless accounts for the extreme penalty of death by
crucifixion. As noted earlier, Tama, as go-between, was liable
also to capital punishment.

BOOK FOUR: OSHICHI THE GREENGROCER'S DAUGHTER

The story of Oshichi excels particularly in its depiction of
adolescent first love. Oshichi's freshness and innocence are felt
all the more, coming directly after the adulterous stories of
Osen and Osan; and even the maiden Onatsu seems a brazen
coquette by comparison. Not that Oshichi is any less passionate
than the other three girls; but rather that love is all so new to
her. Instinct is her sole guide in this, her first and only love.

In the two opening chapters the lovers are brought together
in the midst of disaster; their love flowers timidly, reaching a
consummation only for them to be separated all too soon. Here
it is the maiden Oshichi who forces the final act of love: to her
it is vitally important, in order that they may become really
complete lovers. It is a matter of guileless instinct, set in an
age when the dichotomy of love into the sexual and the platonic
was unknown. At the same time, the reader begins to feel

that extreme absorption and single-mindedness of Oshichi's love, which forms the psychological background for her final act of folly.

The third chapter, featuring one brief meeting with Kichisaburō, shows clearly the despair and longing in Oshichi's heart, and leads directly to her crime and execution in the fourth. Oshichi is fully composed as she is led about the streets of Edo by her executioners; she dies at the stake unwavering, for she never felt her guilt.

Meanwhile Oshichi's young lover became ill and wasted away from longing for her. It was only weeks later that he stumbled upon her grave and learned of her fate. He grieved that he had not joined her sooner. Restrained from suicide, however, he was reminded of his obligations as a samurai, and so had to bide his time until conferring with his protector. When this was done, he entered the priesthood, as Oshichi had hoped he would.[22]

In this novelette Saikaku's attention has lain, not in the development of new facets of the plot, but in the poetic beauty of shy young love and terrible young death. He has told his tale simply, as it actually transpired. There are no artificial or melodramatic elements; and if Oshichi's act of arson seems illogical, it is because her heart had no room for logic on that fateful day.

Sources and background. The execution of the maiden Oshichi took place in Edo in the Third Month of the year 1682, just

---

[22] It was common for a young samurai to have an older samurai as protector and lover. Kichisaburō, as a *rōnin*, i.e., an unemployed samurai, was all the more indebted to his guardian. Kichisaburō's love was thus itself a breach of the ethics of samurai pederasty, though he was perhaps too young to realize the fact. (This development may also have been planned to lead into the pederastic events of Book Five.)

four years before the publication of Saikaku's novel. The most reliable account of Oshichi's story is that found in the *Tenna shōishū,* a miscellaneous record of events that occurred in Edo during the second and third years of the Tenna period, 1682–1683.

According to this source, the fire that dispossessed Oshichi's family broke out on the twenty-eighth day of the Twelfth Month of 1681, at the Daien Temple in Komagome, spreading from there to the Hongō district, and forcing the family to flee to their temple, the Shōsen-in. There, through the mediation of the maidservant Yuki, Oshichi and the temple page Ikuta Shōnosuke became lovers. But soon the family house was rebuilt, and Oshichi was forced to leave the temple. The lovers continued to correspond, and the young page even succeeded once in visiting Oshichi. But after that, unable even to see her lover, Oshichi concluded that if her house were burnt down again they would be able to meet freely. And so on the evening of the second day of the Third Month she tried to set fire to a building nearby but was captured. Oshichi determined not to implicate her lover at any cost. She was paraded around the streets of Edo on the eighteenth day of the same month, in the company of five other arsonists. On the twentieth day she was burned at the stake on the execution grounds of Suzuga-mori. Dressed in fine garments, she met her end bravely, and there were none present who did not mourn her death. Her lover had attempted to appeal to the authorities at the time Oshichi was captured, but was stopped by the maidservant Yuki, who told him of Oshichi's resolution not to implicate him. In the Fourth Month the young man journeyed to the monasteries of Mt. Kōya and there entered the priesthood.

It will be seen that Saikaku's story differs from this semi-historical account only in the addition of minor incidents. He doubtless felt the event impressive enough without elaborations of plot complication, and concentrated his efforts on a poignant retelling of the simple story. Saikaku's main revision lies in the ending, which intensifies and idealizes the lover's emotions and grief.

It is of interest to add that, according to the aforementioned *Tenna shōishū,* in the Second Month of 1682—only a month before Oshichi's death—a maidservant named Ohara, fifteen, from a certain household in the Akasaka district, was paraded through the streets of Edo for the same crime of arson and was then burned at the stake at Suzugamori. Further, as we have seen, five other incendiaries accompanied Oshichi to the stake. It would appear that the crime of arson was very much in vogue at this time, either as a means of personal revenge, or as an outlet for frustrated indignation at the government. Most probably the disastrous fire of late 1681 set off this reaction, one scene of violence suggesting another.

It remains only to record the legal background of Oshichi's punishment:[23]

Regarding sentences for arson: As for the person who sets the fire: Burning at the stake. *However, in a case where no fire results:* Death by decapitation. *As for a person who sets a fire at the direction of another:* Death by decapitation. *However, as for he who gave the direction:* Burning at the stake.

[23] It was the Bakufu government's morbid fear of disorder and social unrest that made the penalties for arson so severe. When we recall the extremely incendiary nature of Japanese cities, and the fact that Edo had already once been completely destroyed in the Great Fire of 1657, the severity of the laws will be more readily understood.

When we recall that Oshichi is still fifteen years of age as Saikaku's novel opens, the following edict lends a particular poignancy to her story:

Even though a fire is set, should the criminal be fourteen years of age or under: Banishment to a distant island. *But when fifteen years of age and over:* Burning at the stake.

From what we know of Oshichi's character, burning was far preferable to lifelong separation from her lover. She would but have echoed the words of Dante's Francesca, to whom she bears so much resemblance:

> *Nessun maggior dolore*
> *Che ricordarsi del tempo felice*
> *Ne la miseria.*

> *There is no greater sorrow*
> *Than to be reminded of a joyous time*
> *While in the midst of misery.*
> —*Inferno,* Canto V

BOOK FIVE: OMAN AND GENGOBEI

Taking his lead from the preceding novelette concerning the fair young *rōnin* Kichisaburō, Saikaku opens the concluding book of *Five Women Who Loved Love* with an intimate picture of the homosexual side of love. The setting is Satsuma, the southernmost province of Japan, a secluded region with its own special customs and dialect and a lively sense of the Spartan code of the samurai. Even Saikaku, though widely traveled, had never penetrated this far south, and an exotic mistiness envelops his depiction of life in this land he had never seen.

The Satsuma samurai—whether justifiably or not—had a reputation for pederasty exceeding that of any other clans, and Saikaku devotes some detail to a description of Gengobei and the joys of "manly love." In the first chapter Gengobei is depicted in an idyllic love scene with his paramour, whose life-flame flickers out before his very eyes. Gengobei enters the priesthood, but on a pilgrimage loses his heart to an even fairer samurai lad. The boy dies before Gengobei's return, but his love is strong enough to bring him back from the dead for one last meeting.[24] This, then—priest, confirmed pederast, and mourner for two dead loves—is the formidable man upon whom the maiden Oman has set her heart!

Here Saikaku pauses for a moment to comment on the fickleness of human beings, whether women or men, in keeping the vows they have made to departed loved ones. Gengobei, however, seriously intends to keep his vows, and it is only the appearance of Oman in the flesh, disguised moreover as a pretty lad, which proves his downfall.[25] Once his passions are aroused, however, even the discovery of Oman's true sex is not enough to

[24] This "return from the dead to meet a loved one" is a venerable theme in Japanese literature, appearing first perhaps as a tale in the eleventh-century *Konjaku monogatari* (Book XXVII, 24). Again in Asai Ryōi's *Otogi-bōko* (1666), Book VI, 3, a similar tale is found, this being an adaptation from Book III of the Chinese collection *Chien-teng hsin-hua*. Both of these sources were doubtless combined by Ueda Akinari when he wrote in his *Ugetsu monogatari* (1768) the story called "Asaji ga yado," utilized effectively in the recent Japanese film *Ugetsu*. All of these stories, however, concern a deceased wife, whose affectionate spirit reappears briefly to greet her husband's homecoming.

[25] Oman's masquerade was not so bizarre as it may appear to the modern reader. The actresses in the earlier Women's Kabuki had often played men's parts; and after women were banned from the stage, fair boys took the roles of women. In Saikaku's time there was a

deter Gengobei, and he is summarily converted to normal ways of love. In the final chapter the lovers are made to suffer for a time, but in the end they receive their reward of wealth and joy.

In the story of Oman and Gengobei will be found the only happy ending in this volume. Although such might facetiously be considered but a proper reward for Oman's determination against all odds to get her man, actually this is quite in keeping with the theatrical conventions of the time.

The division of each story into five chapters has been explained in terms of the Nō drama, but in fact, it is the five-act form of the contemporary Jōruri drama that was most probably Saikaku's source.[26] For although Saikaku possessed a considerable and detailed knowledge of the Nō, it was only the year before this that he himself had written two Jōruri plays, both in five acts. Further, the inclusion of five separate stories in the volume itself may perhaps reflect this convention. With these factors in mind, the completion of the series with a comedy is clearly seen to reflect current theatrical conventions. The reader leaves the book with a temporarily light heart, free to ponder the preceding four tragedies at his leisure.[27]

In addition, it will be seen that this last story is the only one where no crime is involved and where the lovers are on an

special class of harlots who dressed as young men and plied their trade among Buddhist priests—who preferred not be seen with women!

[26] As noted above, the anti-novelistic *michiyuki* sequence in Book III. 3, is itself a theatrical intrusion.

[27] This type of arrangement is also reminiscent of the methods employed in the linked-verse composition of the period, where the final verse aimed at making manifest the camaraderie of the group of poets. This final verse (called the *ageku*) always took Spring for its theme whatever the season employed in the preceding verses. When successful, it vibrantly concluded and bound together the series.

entirely equal level. All of these factors doubtless influenced
Saikaku in his choice of a happy conclusion, where the actual
event appears to have ended in the suicide of both lovers.[28]

Sources and background. The only factual information we
possess regarding this story appears in a chronology of the
mid-nineteenth century, which simply records: "1663: In Satsuma, the love-suicide of Gengobei and Oman." Besides this,
there is only the reference in the passage of Chikamatsu's drama
on the subject, *The Song of Satsuma (Satsuma-uta),* of 1704:
"It is said to be some time around Kambun...."[29]

Gengobei was also the subject of a humorous popular song of
the period. This song, extant only in fragments, is quoted first
in the poet Bashō's *Kai-ōi* of 1672, then in Saikaku's novel, and
finally in Chikamatsu's drama. It refers humorously to Gengobei's penniless condition: "With a scabbard worth *three*
cents, a sword-knot worth *two* cents, and inside, a piece of
rough-hewn cypress wood." The original Gengobei may well
have been one of the *otokodate* townsman-gallants of Edo—
probably a native of Satsuma—whose personality subsequently
became linked in the popular theatre with the story of Oman.

It is thus impossible to ascertain the extent of Saikaku's
knowledge of the actual events in the story of Oman and Gengobei. It seems probable that he had few specific details to
work from, and handled the story freely—the more so in that
it was an event of more than twenty years earlier, set in a distant
and little-known province.

[28] Saikaku treats of love-suicide but once in all his works, in *A
Mirror of the Beauties* (1684). There he makes his disapproval of the
practice clear. To him it was neither a sign of great love, nor even
of repentance for past sins, but rather an indication of weakness and
defeat.

[29] T.岩 Kambun period dates from 1661 to 1673.

*   *   *

Having examined the background of these five novelettes, a
certain symmetry will be observed. The first and last stories
are events of a generation earlier than the time of writing, and
both occur in outlying provinces. The middle three stories treat
events close to the time of writing and take as their setting the
three major cities of Japan—Osaka, Kyoto, and Edo, this latter
order itself reflecting the relative interests of an inhabitant of
Osaka, as was Saikaku.

There is perhaps no profound meaning in these deductions,
but they do reflect Saikaku's strong feeling for the regionalism
of Japan. And to the readers of his day, this element of chang-
ing local color added much to the interest of the stories, in
somewhat the same manner as had that in his volume of *Tales
from the Provinces* of the year before.[30] It is not impossible
that the whole idea of the work may have grown out of some
such tales-from-the-provinces concept, i.e., the depiction of a
famous love story from each of five varied locales. This would
explain why Osaka, the life and scandals of which Saikaku knew
best, was limited to one story, whereas semi-legendary tales
were introduced from such distant provinces as Harima and
Satsuma.

Five Women Who Loved Love marks the first appearance
in Japanese literature of the bourgeois woman as a dominant
heroine—an innovation that was to have reverberations throughout later Edo literature. Hitherto in Japanese fiction it was

[30] This geographical element is reflected also in the covers of the
five slim volumes which comprise *Five Women Who Loved Love*, each of
which, at the top of the titleslip, gives the name of the locale, together with the profession involved—cooper, almanac maker, greengrocer
—or some other distinguishing feature.

largely the courtesan heroine who took an active role in love. From Saikaku's lead, whole schools of the novel developed with ordinary townswomen as their love heroines.[31]

Certainly one of the notable features of *Five Women Who Loved Love* is Saikaku's depiction of women as taking the decisive role in love affairs. This approach is particularly striking with the three maidens of fifteen, who see the man they want and immediately go about getting him. In none of these stories is the hero of any great stature: it is the girl who directs the action, and most often takes the tragic consequences. The two young wives, though not exactly beginning their adulterous affairs of their own accord, are nonetheless ready enough to accept the pleasures and horrors of their fate once the die is cast.

Even taking into account the young age of the three maidens,[32] Saikaku's view of woman's predominant part in love affairs is certainly a valid one, though it may at first seem surprising in a feudal and strictly anti-feminist society. Saikaku's women, though quite romantic, are still frank enough about the part that sex plays in their desire to meet their lovers.

To realize the uniqueness of Saikaku's bold and sympathatic treatment, it is necessary to remember that each of these loves

[31] See particularly the *Yomihon* genre of the mid-eighteenth century and following. Plebeian heroines had occasionally appeared prior to Saikaku, as in the atypical *Zeraku monogatari* (ca. 1659) and in pre-feudal romances such as *The Tale of Genji;* but none of these women played an active role in the story development. From the 1660's on, courtesans came to take an increasingly dominant place in fiction, but these women formed a class in themselves, quite separate from the bourgeoisie.

[32] As in Renaissance Europe, the age of fifteen or sixteen was considered fully mature for a girl, and marriages were often effected earlier. Shakespeare's Juliet was fourteen ; Boccaccio's "Patient Griselda," twelve.

was a crime against feudal law. Even to write sympathetically about such was perilous; for although at this period the Edo government concerned itself little about pornography, anything that savored of anti-authoritarianism or lese majesty was an unpardonable crime. Ample grounds could have been found for stamping this volume criminal, simply on account of its sympathetic depiction of creatures who had violated the most sacred laws of feudalism.

The basis of the feudal system lay in the strict maintenance of hierarchy. Thus, there was no simple crime of seduction, abduction, elopement, rape, or murder: the criminality lay in the comparative rank of the doer and the victim. Legalized murder was, it is true, a privilege only of the samurai, and even for them, it was legitimate only toward persons of lower rank or class, and on at least technical provocation. The other acts of violence, however, might well have gone unpunished in a townsman employer toward an employee. When the ranks were reversed, the punishment was death.

Of all Saikaku's works of fiction *Five Women Who Loved Love* features perhaps the greatest complexity of plot and character development. This doubtless reflects the influence of the earlier dramatic versions upon which he drew for material and incident. Saikaku's forte was never plot, but style; and thus much of the interest of his stylistically greatest works must remain obscure to the Western reader. The present tales, however, may be enjoyed by all.

BIBLIOGRAPHICAL NOTE

Kōshoku gonin onna was published in Osaka in the Second Month of 1686, in five slim quarto volumes. The illustrations were by Yoshida Hambei, the leading illustrator of the Kyoto-Osaka region. The first edition comprises two printings, the first Osaka, the second combined Osaka and Edo. In the mid-eighteenth century the work was republished under the title *Tōsei onna katagi (Types of Modern Women),* and enjoyed considerable popularity, being twice reprinted. Facsimile editions are available in full size (5 vols., Tokyo, 1929), and in reduced offset (1 vol., Tokyo, 1946), and the retitled edition in a mimeographed reproduction (Tokyo, 1922). First editions will be found in the collections of Tenri University, Kyoto University, Ueno Library, Waseda University, British Museum, Bibliothèque Nationale, Edogawa Rampo, and the present writer. Kyoto University, Tōyō Bunko, Okada Shin, and Yokoyama Shigeru possess copies of the retitled edition. Modern reprints are available in at least a dozen different editions; particularly to be recommended as unexpurgated and most accurate is the text in Volume II of the *Teihon Saikaku zenshū* (Complete Works of Saikaku: Standard Edition), published at Tokyo in 1949.

Other TUT BOOKS available:

SUN-DIALS AND ROSES OF YESTERDAY *by Alice Morse Earle*

THE TEN FOOT SQUARE HUT AND TALES OF THE HEIKE: Being Two Thirteenth-century Japanese classics, the "Hojoki" and selections from the "Heike Monogatari" *translated by A. L. Sadler*

THE TOURIST AND THE REAL JAPAN *by Boye de Mente*

TYPHOON! TYPHOON! An Illustrated Haiku Sequence *by Lucile M. Bogue*

UNBEATEN TRACKS IN JAPAN: An Account of Travels in the Interior Including Visits to the Aborigines of Yezo and the Shrine of Nikko *by Isabella L. Bird*

Please order from your bookstore or write directly to:

CHARLES E. TUTTLE CO., INC.
Suido 1-chome, 2–6, Bunkyo-ku, Tokyo 112

or:

CHARLES E. TUTTLE CO., INC.
Rutland, Vermont 05701 U.S.A.